Simply Spirit
READING ● HEALING CENTER

1304 Meador Avenue,
Bellingham, WA 9
360-647-7134

D0978767

THE X-FACTOR

Getting Extraordinary Results from Ordinary People

ROSS R. RECK, Ph.D.

John Wiley & Sons, Inc.

New York • Chichester • Weinheim • Brisbane • Singapore • Toronto

Published by John Wiley & Sons, Inc.

Published simultaneously in Canada.

This publication is designed to provide accurate and authoritative
information in regard to the subject matter covered. It is sold with the
understanding that the publisher is not engaged in rendering legal,
accounting, or other professional services. If legal advice or other expert
assistance is required, the services of a competent professional person
should be sought.

Library of Congress Cataloging-in-Publication Data

Reck, Ross Richard, 1945–
    The X-Factor : getting extraordinary results from ordinary
people / Ross R. Reck.
       p. cm.
    Includes index.
    ISBN 0-471-44389-1 (cloth : alk. paper)
    1. Employee motivation.   I. Title.
HF5549.5.M63 R43   2001
658.3'14—dc21   2001026648

Printed in the United States of America.

10 9 8 7 6 5 4 3 2 1

To Marcia, Philip, Katie, and Nancy,
the best family anyone could ever have

Acknowledgments

Mary Norfleet, my long-time partner, for her tremendous support and encouragement.

Brian Long, my coauthor on *The Win-Win Negotiator*, for his contributions in developing the PRAM Model.

Jim Woodson for helping me see the world through a clearer set of eyes.

Tom Peters and Bob Waterman for their breakthrough book, *In Search of Excellence*, which inspired the fifteen years of research that went into *The X-Factor*.

Joyce Kinicki for putting me on the path that eventually led to the discovery of the X-Factor.

Kevin Freiberg and Jackie Freiberg, authors of *NUTS!*, for showing the world what the heart and soul of a well-run company (Southwest Airlines) looks like.

Douglas McGregor, author of *The Human Side of Enterprise*, for making the case that management is 100% about people.

Dale Carnegie, author of *How To Win Friends And Influence People*, and Samuel A. Culbert, author of *Mind-Set Management*, for corroborating the fact that self-interest is the only thing that motivates human behavior.

Viktor Frankl, author of *Man's Search For Meaning*, for pointing out the powerful role that meaning plays in determining an individual's self-interest.

W. Edwards Demming, the quality icon, for showing me the difference between a satisfied customer and a loyal customer.

Glenn Buege of Glenn Buege Buick in Lansing, Michigan, for teaching me, first hand, the important role that a reminder system plays in the consistent execution of the basics.

Marcia Reck, my wife, for her constant encouragement and willingness to proofread on demand throughout the duration of this project.

Breathing life into a project like *The X-Factor* requires a coordinated team effort. Individuals who played key roles include:

Sally Kur, of the Kur Carr Group for her initial editing of the manuscript; Jo Fagan, literary agent, from Jane Dystel Literary Management; the team from John Wiley & Sons, especially Karen Hansen, editor, and her able assistant, Kirsten Miller, along with Amy Levy, Marketing, Alison Bamberger, publicity, and Associate Managing Editor, Linda Indig; Cathy Lewis, publicist, from C.S. Lewis & Co.; Mary Ellen Langlois, speaking agent, from Platform Speakers International; and the staff of Cape Cod Compositors, for their painstaking efforts in editing and proofreading the manuscript.

Contents

vii

Introduction

Southwest Airlines is one of the most respected and admired American businesses, and for good reason. In their excellent book about the airline titled *Nuts!* Kevin and Jackie Freiberg point out that Southwest has managed to earn a profit every year since 1973 (while charging the lowest fares), and its profit margins are the highest in the industry. Since 1978, more than one hundred airlines have gone bankrupt. During that time Southwest continued to expand and is still growing at a rate of 20 to 30 percent annually. Southwest dominates its markets with a market share of 60 percent or better in almost every nonstop city-pair market it serves. Its workforce is the most loyal and productive in the industry and has the lowest turnover rate. Labor relations at Southwest are among the best even though most of its employees are union members. During the Gulf War in 1990, employees voluntarily contributed $150,000 from their paychecks to help the company buy fuel as prices skyrocketed.

There's still more. Southwest has the best customer service record in the industry based on baggage handling, on-time performance, and customer complaints. In addition, Southwest cancels the smallest percentage of flights of any airline and has the best safety record in the industry.

The Southwest Airlines story is truly remarkable, and it's not over yet. During the past decade, its story has been analyzed, documented, and reported by numerous management authors, scholars, and gurus to the point where there is little, if anything, we don't know concerning how Southwest conducts its affairs. With all this information on one of America's best-run companies, one has to ask the question: How come there aren't more companies with a track record like that of Southwest Airlines?

The answer to this question is quite simple: The management at Southwest focuses its attention on those managerial activities that produce *extraordinary* results. Most other companies focus their attention on those managerial activities that produce *ordinary* results. The difference between ordinary and extraordinary results is depicted in the following comparison:

A *Ordinary Results*	B *Extraordinary Results*
Customers who shop for the lowest price	Customers who enthusiastically pay premium prices
Barely surviving in a highly competitive market	Dominating a highly competitive market
Implementing the newest management fad	Getting your current management system to work
Having to cold call new customers	New customers who call you
Suppliers who fill orders	Suppliers who show you how to reduce costs
Employees who resist change	Employees who suggest change
Tension between labor and management	A 15-year labor agreement with double-digit productivity gains

Which set of managerial results would you like to achieve? If you choose Column "B," you identify yourself as someone who prefers taking charge and making things happen rather than following the crowd. You no·doubt aspire to achieve far beyond what most people would consider acceptable or good. You are not interested in small or incremental results; you want extraordinary results and are willing to work exceptionally hard to accomplish them.

Hard work, however, does not guarantee extraordinary managerial results. You also have to know how to *manage*. Herein lies the problem. Just how do you manage in order to make the kinds of results listed in Column "B" become routine and commonplace?

Over the years, researchers have published tens of thousands of studies dealing with the different aspects of managing, such as motivation, rewards, goal setting, organization structure, job satisfaction, performance measurement, and so forth. In addition, there are hundreds of textbooks dealing with the subject of management, as well as thousands of trade books. To date, however, none of these studies or books has produced a coherent system that will enable a manager to achieve Column "B" type results regularly.

The state of the art in management today is analogous to a large jigsaw puzzle with pieces scattered everywhere. The fact that no one is really sure which of these scattered pieces is relevant makes solving the puzzle impossible.

The X-Factor is about solving this management puzzle. It's about identifying all the relevant pieces and then fitting them tightly together to form a *complete* system that will enable any manager to achieve the kind of results depicted in Column "B" on a consistent and continual basis. Presented at the end of this book are a number of real-world examples of companies and individuals who have successfully used this system. These examples illustrate how you, too, can use this system to achieve your own set of extraordinary results.

Ross R. Reck, Ph.D.

In Search of a Great Manager

Phil Ross is a very bright man in his mid-30s who has developed into a very good manager. His long-term goal is to become a *great* manager; he wants to be the president of his company one day.

Over the years, Phil has rigorously pursued his own personal development program. He has attended numerous workshops dealing with various management topics—team building, motivation, empowerment, consensus building, problem solving, and labor relations. He religiously reads the *Harvard Business Review, Business Week,* and *The Wall Street Journal,* as well as nearly every best-selling business book as soon as it becomes available. Phil eagerly admits enjoying these activities and the learning that has come from them. Recently, however, he began to experience a growing sense of frustration.

"How is it," Phil asked himself, "that after 10 years of attending management workshops and reading everything I can get my hands on, I still don't feel that I fully understand what management is all about? Is it me, or is it that these lecturers and authors I've been exposed to don't fully understand what managing is all about?"

Phil's questioning and restlessness continued at work for weeks. Again and again he pondered the same question: "What don't I get about this whole management issue? I know most of the jargon. I practice much of what I have learned. My team is in a good productive mode. But I am not growing."

One evening while searching through his library for an answer to a management concern, he had an inspiration. "I know what it is! Management is like a large jigsaw puzzle with pieces scattered everywhere. While each of the lecturers and authors I've been exposed to seem to understand one or more pieces of the puzzle, none of them understand *all* the pieces, much less how they fit together. If I'm ever going to understand fully what management is all about, I'm going to have to find all the pieces to this puzzle and solve it myself!"

The next day Phil created his own research project. He decided to interview a large number of management experts—presidents of successful companies along with some of their top-level managers, as well as leading academics, consultants, and authors in management and related fields. "Surely," Phil thought, "with something as complicated as putting people into outer space having become routine, finding the pieces to the management puzzle and solving it shouldn't be all that difficult."

The results of Phil's research project proved very interesting. While most of the people he interviewed agreed with the idea that managing was a matter of getting things done through other people, none of them agreed on a best way to do it. One successful company president told him, "To be a successful manager, you have to create a win-win situation with your employees." Another said, "The name of the game in management is to drive out fear and create an atmosphere of trust among your employees. If you do this, results will take care of themselves."

A leading academic told Phil, "Effective managing is a function of developing proper individual or team performance measures and then monitoring these measures closely." On the other hand, several leading authors strongly subscribed to the idea that "Successful management is a matter of empowering your employees to do the job and then supporting them in their efforts."

The consultants he interviewed also had their own brands of advice. One prominent consultant felt strongly that "Managing is a matter of wandering around among your employees, being visible, staying in touch, and promoting informal communication. I'm not exactly sure why this works; it just does." Another leading consultant took a different approach: "If you hire good people in the first place, you are well on your way to being a successful manager."

Phil was both disappointed and amazed by the results of his research project. He was disappointed in that he felt no closer to solving the management puzzle than he was before the project started. He was amazed that so many people who claimed to be management authorities, experts, and gurus simply weren't what they claimed to be. While each of them appeared to understand one or more small pieces of the management puzzle, none of them had a solid grasp of the big picture—how the pieces fit together.

Phil was stumped. He was not about to give up on his quest to solve the management puzzle, but he had no idea how to proceed.

After dinner one evening, Phil settled in to

watch the evening news. As he gazed at the television, he continued to ponder his lack of success in solving the management puzzle. Then a feature story caught his attention. The story was about a man named Sam Wharton, who was president of a large manufacturing company headquartered in a nearby city.

Mr. Wharton had taken over as president of the company 10 years earlier. At that time, the company was in a shambles and in serious danger of closing its doors for good. Market share was at an all-time low, productivity gains were nonexistent, the union was on strike, and employee loyalty was a thing of the past.

Today, the company was experiencing record profits. In fact, the company had been profitable every quarter for the past eight years. In addition, the company was experiencing double-digit productivity gains thanks to the commitment of its unionized employees. Employee morale and loyalty were at all-time highs, and the company now dominated its industry in terms of market share.

The reason for the feature story was that Sam Wharton was on his way to the White House to participate in a conference on corporate responsibility. His company had been recognized by the president of the United States as an Outstanding Corporate Citizen.

"In the short time we have left, can you share

with our viewers the secret to your firm's success?" asked the reporter.

"I'd be happy to," responded Mr. Wharton. "It's something I refer to as the **X-Factor**. Over the years, I have learned that excited people produce extraordinary results. So, the managers at my company and I get our people excited, and we keep them that way."

"How do you pull this off?" asked the reporter.

"We simply give people what they are looking for in their jobs," responded Mr. Wharton.

"What a fascinating answer," said the reporter. "Thank you so much for your time."

"Thank *you*," said Mr. Wharton.

Phil was very interested. "I need to talk to Sam Wharton. Maybe his X-Factor holds the key to solving the management puzzle."

The next morning, Phil called Mr. Wharton's company.

"Good morning. Sam Wharton's office, Mary speaking. How may I help you?"

"Hello, my name is Phil Ross. I saw Mr. Wharton on television last night and was hoping I might be able to meet with him to talk about the X-Factor— anytime at his convenience."

"I know Sam would be very happy to talk to you," responded Mary. "He's very busy, but he'll always find a little time to talk to someone about the X-Factor. He has an opening Thursday morning at 9:30."

"That would be perfect," replied Phil.

"I'll schedule you for an hour," said Mary. "That should give you plenty of time."

"Thank you so much."

"See you next Thursday."

Meeting a Great Manager

P hil arrived a few minutes early for his scheduled appointment with Mr. Wharton and was
warmly greeted by Mary. He couldn't help but
notice that she was wearing a pin shaped like an X
on her jacket lapel.

"You must be Phil Ross," she said as she stood up
to shake his hand.

"Yes, I am," he replied.

"I'm very happy to meet you. Sam is still at his X-Meeting, but he should be back shortly."

"An X-Meeting? May I ask what an X-Meeting is?" inquired Phil.

"Each department, group, or team begins each day with a short meeting that we refer to as an X-Meeting," Mary responded. "The purpose of these daily meetings is to make sure that we've still got the X-Factor under control. I'm sure Sam will fill you in on the details. While you're waiting, could I get you a cup of coffee or a soft drink?"

"A soft drink would be great," replied Phil.

While Mary was away getting the beverage, Phil had a chance to collect his thoughts. "They really take this X-Factor business seriously around here," he said to himself. "I can't wait to find out what it is."

"Here's your soft drink," Mary said. "Sam should be here any second."

Just then a man in his mid-50s, wearing an X-shaped pin on his jacket lapel, walked through the door. "You must be Phil Ross," he said as he reached out to shake his hand.

"Yes, I am, and I'm very pleased to meet you, Mr. Wharton."

"Just call me Sam. Tell me, what can I do for you?"

Phil explained that he felt he was a very capable manager, but he wanted to become a great manager, even president of his company one day. He went on to tell Sam about his personal development program.

"Let me guess," said Sam. "With every workshop you attended and every book or article you read, you came away with one or more very useful ideas, but you never came away with the big picture."

"Exactly!" exclaimed Phil. "But how did you know?"

"I had the same experience myself," replied Sam.

Phil then went on to explain his research project where he interviewed a number of management experts in an attempt to find all the pieces to the management puzzle and solve it.

"Let me guess again," interrupted Sam. "You're no closer to solving your puzzle now than you were before you started your project."

"That's right," responded Phil. "That's why I called you. I'm hoping the X-Factor you mentioned during your television interview either is the solution to the management puzzle or can at least shed some additional light on how to solve it."

"Phil, I am impressed. I made the same journey myself a number of years ago, and I can appreciate your frustration. In my case, though, I was fortunate enough to trip over the solution to the management puzzle—although at the time I didn't know it."

"Wait a minute!" exclaimed Phil. "Did you say that you've solved the management puzzle, that you understand the big picture of what management is all about?"

"Absolutely!" replied Sam. "That's why my company is so successful."

"Are you willing to share it with me?" asked Phil.

"Certainly," responded Sam. "Let's start by building upon what you've already learned. When you conducted your interviews with those management experts, was there anything that these people agreed on?"

"They all pretty much agreed that managing is a matter of getting things done through other people," said Phil.

"That's a good place to start," acknowledged Sam. He then walked over to a large chart hung on the wall behind his desk. The chart was divided into two columns—"A" and "B." "Take a few moments and read this," he said.

The chart read:

A	B
Customers who shop for the lowest price	Customers who enthusiastically pay premium prices
Barely surviving in a highly competitive market	Dominating a highly competitive market
Implementing the newest management fad	Getting your current management system to work
Having to cold call new customers	New customers who call you
Suppliers who fill orders	Suppliers who show you how to reduce costs
Employees who resist change	Employees who suggest change
Tension between labor and management	A 15-year labor agreement with double digit productivity gains

When Phil had finished reading the chart, Sam asked, "Which of the two sets of results would you like to achieve, 'A' or 'B'?"

"Why, Column 'B,' of course."

"Exactly," agreed Sam with a smile. "Everyone would like to achieve the kinds of results listed in Column 'B.' Yet Column 'A' pretty accurately depicts the kinds of results most commonly associated with people who would describe themselves as *good* managers. I refer to these as *ordinary* results. Column 'B,' on the other hand, represents *extraordinary* results. These are the kinds of results achieved by *great* managers."

Sam paused, then went on, "The common definition of managing—getting things done through other people—simply doesn't tell you what you need to know to become a great manager."

"Then how do you become a great manager?"

"You have to learn to *tame* the X-Factor," declared Sam.

"What is the X-Factor?" asked Phil.

CHAPTER

3

Discovering the X-Factor

S am smiled as he walked over to a blank flip chart, picked up a marker, and began to write. When he finished, the chart read:

THE X-FACTOR

GETTING ORDINARY PEOPLE X-CITED ABOUT
GOING THE X-TRA MILE TO HELP YOU, THE
MANAGER, ACHIEVE X-TRAORDINARY RESULTS

"I see why you call it the X-Factor," declared Phil. "This X-Factor takes things so much further than the common definition of management. Instead of merely being concerned with getting things done, which can easily lead to ordinary results, the X-Factor focuses directly on achieving extraordinary results."

"You're catching on," observed Sam.

"This sounds very exciting," said Phil. "But I have no idea how to make the X-Factor happen."

"That's what *taming* the X-Factor is all about," replied Sam.

"All right then, how do I go about taming the X-Factor?"

"Before we can talk about taming or harnessing the X-Factor, you need to understand the basic elements that make up the X-Factor." Once again Sam walked over to his flip chart. When he finished writing, the chart read:

BASIC ELEMENTS OF THE X-FACTOR

- PEOPLE
- MOTIVATION

Sam motioned Phil toward the chart. "When it comes to achieving extraordinary results," he said, "these are the only two things that really matter—regardless of the level of managing you're talking about."

Sam went on, "Let's look at the first of these elements, people. Taming the X-Factor is 100 percent about people and nothing else! If you ever expect to achieve extraordinary results as a manager, you must first realize that people are your most important resource. You can't achieve extraordinary results by yourself; you need all the help you can get."

"Don't most people in managerial positions already know this?" asked Phil.

"They do and they don't," responded Sam. "Most managers, including those who would describe themselves as good managers, pay a great deal of lip service to this notion; but, in reality, they give very little attention to their people. Great managers, on the other hand, take this people business very seriously. They truly realize that it's people, not capital investment and automation, that bring about quality improvements and productivity gains. Furthermore, they realize that people are the only true source of creativity, innovation, and new ideas. As far as these great managers are concerned, people take precedence over everything else in a business organization, including systems, organization charts, strategy, numbers, rules, procedures, and titles."

"So," said Phil, "managers who achieve extraordinary results are those who maximize their involvement with their people."

"You are exactly right," said Sam, "and I'll explain why in just a minute. But first, let's talk about the other basic element of the X-Factor, which is motivation. Appreciating the fact that people are your most important resource is not enough by itself to achieve extraordinary managerial results; you also have to know what motivates them or gets them excited. Tell me, from reading all those management books, attending all those workshops, and interviewing all those experts, what did you learn about human motivation?"

Phil paused. "I'm embarrassed to admit that after all that, I still don't really understand what human motivation is all about."

"Don't be embarrassed," said Sam. "Most managers don't understand what human motivation is all about, and that's because the people who write about it and talk about it don't understand it either. If these so-called management experts really understood human motivation, we wouldn't have all these gimmicky management fads coming out every time you turn around."

"For not knowing what they're talking about, these management experts sure have a lot to say," commented Phil. "I mean, there are hundreds of books and thousands of articles and workshops on the subject."

"There sure are," responded Sam. "Researchers

have tried to find a cause-and-effect linkage between nearly everything under the sun and human
motivation. For example, they've tried to assess
the impact that such things as goals, satisfaction,
intrinsic and extrinsic rewards, autonomy, positive
reinforcement, meaningful work, and the like have
on individual motivation. Why, they have even
taken some of the things they've learned in labora-
tory experiments with rats and thrown them into
the motivational hopper. But instead of clearing
up the motivational picture, what these so-called
experts have created, to borrow a phrase from
William James, is 'one great blooming, buzzing
confusion.' "

"It sounds like there's a motivational puzzle that's
a subset of the management puzzle that I'm trying to
solve," said Phil.

"Right you are," replied Sam, "That is, if you listen to the experts. In reality, human motivation is
not at all complicated or confusing. When you get
right down to it, all people, including you and me,
are motivated by one thing and one thing only."

"What's that?" asked Phil.

Sam then walked over to his flip chart and wrote:

SELF-INTEREST

"Self-interest?" questioned Phil. "That sounds pretty mercenary. Isn't that the same thing as selfishness?"

"Not at all," replied Sam. "*Selfishness* is the excessive concern for one's own welfare without regard for others. If, as a manager, you take seriously the notion that people are your most important resource, there is no room for selfish behavior."

"Then what is self-interest?" asked Phil.

"It's part of human nature," responded Sam. "You see, every one of us is born with a fundamental desire to satisfy our basic human needs: safety, security, belonging, feeling good about ourselves, and being in control of our lives. These are the bedrock concerns of all human beings, which means they are extremely powerful motivators. Furthermore, each individual has a unique personal agenda concerning which needs are important and the ways in which he or she prefers to satisfy those needs. This unique agenda is a person's self-interest."

"This sounds like the Need Theory of Motivation," said Phil. "Haven't we known about self-interest for a long time?"

"Yes, we have," replied Sam, "but we haven't taken it seriously because we've never fully appreciated the powerful role it plays in determining an individual's behavior. When it comes to motivating people, self-interest is the *only* thing that matters.

For this reason, people are constantly searching for opportunities to further their self-interest; and when they come across these opportunities, they become very excited."

"What you are saying is that self-interest is the driving force behind people's behavior."

"Absolutely," responded Sam.

"So, I need to home in on the self-interests of my people if I expect to achieve extraordinary results."

"That's right," replied Sam. "You must accept as fact that people come to work motivated to pursue *their* self-interests, not yours. Furthermore, you must realize that no matter how hard you try, you cannot change or otherwise modify an individual's self-interest to make it like yours. Instead, you have to accept it for what it is and learn to *engage* it."

"What do you mean by 'engage it'?" asked Phil.

"You must find a way to connect the respective self-interests of your people with your self-interest," responded Sam. "Let me illustrate with a simple example."

Sam opened the top drawer of his desk and pulled out two five-by-seven-inch cards. He handed the cards to Phil and said, "I picked up these from two hotels that I stayed at recently. I want you to take a moment and read each of them." The cards read:

Dear Guest:

The management of this hotel would greatly appreciate it if you would consider reusing your towels a second day. This would greatly help us reduce our operating costs. Please place any towels that you are willing to reuse back on the rack. This will tell housekeeping not to replace them.

Thank you very much.

Sincerely,
The Management

Dear Guest:

As a responsible citizen, you are probably concerned about doing your part to help preserve our fragile environment. If you are, the management of this hotel would like to suggest a way that you could make a real difference. Every year, millions of tons of detergent pollute our environment through the laundering of hotel towels that really don't need to be laundered. This is where *you* can help. If you are willing to reuse your towels, simply place them back on the rack. This will tell housekeeping not to replace them.

Thank you so much for doing your part in keeping our planet green.

Sincerely,
The Management

"Which card do you think motivated me to reuse my towels?" queried Sam.

"Why, the second one," replied Phil.

"What makes you think that?"

"With the first card, the hotel management dealt only with its self-interest, which was reducing its costs," responded Phil. "There was nothing in it for you."

"Exactly!" exclaimed Sam. "That's why I didn't feel overly compelled to reuse my towels in that hotel. Doing so would have only put money in the hotel's coffers, with me getting nothing in return."

"The second card," continued Phil, "began by addressing something you were interested in—doing your part to preserve the environment. Who can disagree with such a noble cause? The card then went on to tell you how you could contribute to this cause with almost no effort on your part. I'll bet you reused your towels in this hotel, didn't you?"

"I sure did," replied Sam. "And I felt good about myself while doing so."

"I think I'm starting to see the relationship between motivation and self-interest," said Phil. "The intent of both cards was the same. The management of both hotels wanted *your* help in reducing *their* costs. The first card failed in its attempt to motivate you because it dealt only with the hotel management's self-interest. There was nothing in it for you. The second card succeeded in motivating you to help reduce that hotel's costs because it dealt with your self-interest. The self-interest of that hotel's management was never addressed. I'll bet that second card actually got you a little excited about putting money in that particular hotel's pocket."

Sam smiled. "Pretty *extraordinary*, don't you think?"

"I'll say," agreed Phil. "What's even more amazing to me is that it took no more effort to get you excited about helping one of the hotels reduce its costs than it did to turn you off about doing so for the other hotel."

"Right you are, " said Sam. "Achieving extraordinary results as a manager is not so much a matter of hard work; it's a matter of doing certain things right."

"You know," said Phil, "this relationship between motivation and self-interest is very similar to something I read in Douglas McGregor's book called *The Human Side of Enterprise*.* McGregor said something to the effect that the job of a manager is to create a set of conditions such that the members of the organization perceive that they can achieve their own goals *best* by directing their efforts toward the success of the enterprise. That's exactly what that second hotel card was all about! It took the hotel's self-interest, which was reducing costs, and connected it to your self-interest, which was pre-

*Douglas McGregor, *The Human Side of Enterprise* (New York: McGraw-Hill, 1960).

serving the environment. As a result, the more you pursued your self-interest, the more money you saved the hotel."

"That book was first published in 1960," said Sam, "and Douglas McGregor was right. Unfortunately, his idea never really caught on."

"Why not?" asked Phil.

"Simply put," explained Sam, "McGregor couldn't figure out how to put his idea into action effectively."

"I'll bet you've figured out how to implement McGregor's idea, haven't you?" said Phil.

"That's what taming the X-Factor is all about," replied Sam.

CHAPTER

4

R$_x$ for Taming the X-Factor

S am then pointed to a framed poster behind his desk. The poster looked like this:

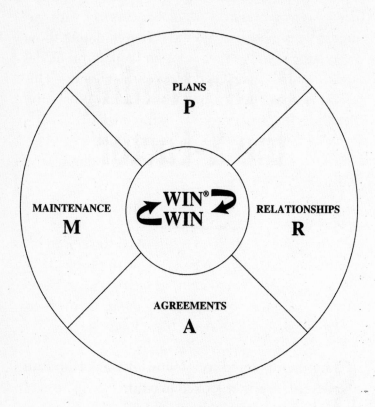

The PRAM Model
R_x for Taming the X-Factor

"I came across this model in a book called *The Win-Win Negotiator** right after I took over as president of this company," said Sam. "My first major task as president was to negotiate a new labor contract with our union. This model served me very well during those negotiations, and as time went on I found this model applied to managing every facet of the business. This model is what I use to tame the X-Factor. What's the first thing that strikes you about this model?"

"It's circular in shape," answered Phil.

"What does that circle tell you about taming the X-Factor?" asked Sam.

"That it's a continuous, ongoing process," responded Phil.

"That's right," affirmed Sam. "And the reason it's continuous is that you are dealing with people. People are sensitive, have delicate egos, and are very concerned about feeling good about themselves. They don't like being treated like light switches."

"Light switches?"

"Turn them on when you need their help and then ignore them until you need their help again," replied Sam. "If you treat people this way, you send them a very clear message that you are taking them for granted. Once people receive this message, they become turned off about going the extra mile for

*Ross R. Reck, Ph.D. and Brian G. Long, Ph.D., *The Win-Win Negotiator: How to Negotiate Favorable Agreements That Last* (New York: Pocket Books, 1989).

you, and they take their best efforts to where they are better appreciated."

"Let me see if I understand this," said Phil. "If the people who work for you feel that you are taking them for granted, achieving extraordinary results as a manager could become very difficult."

"Try 'impossible,' " said Sam. "It simply can't happen if your people think you take them for granted." He paused for a moment, then asked, "What else strikes you about this model?"

"The words 'WIN-WIN' in the center of the model," responded Phil.

"Why do you suppose 'win-win' is at the heart of taming the X-Factor?"

Phil thought for a moment, then suggested, "As a manager, I want the people who work for me to get excited about helping me achieve extraordinary results. These extraordinary results represent the self-interest that I'm pursuing—or my 'win,' if you will. Since the people who work for me are also motivated out of self-interest, before I can expect them to get excited about helping me achieve these results, I first have to find a 'win' in it for them to do so. In other words, I have to create a situation where the people who work for me view pursuing my self-interest (extraordinary results) as the best way for them to pursue their own self-interests."

Phil paused, then blurted out, "Wait a minute! Isn't this what Douglas McGregor said the job of a manager should be? And isn't this how that hotel got you excited about reusing your towels?"

"Brilliant," declared Sam with a smile. "You see, every aspect of taming the X-Factor has to be win-win; that's why it's at the core of the model. If your approach to dealing with the people who work for you is not win-win, there is no self-interest for them to pursue only your self-interest. As we discussed earlier when we talked about motivation, people get very excited about pursuing their own self-interests, but they really don't care about pursuing someone else's. Consequently, if your approach to managing is not win-win, the *best* results you can hope for are ordinary results."

"I'm beginning to see now why there aren't more great managers," said Phil. "Since most managers don't take seriously the notion that people are their most important resource, there is no reason for them to think win-win. As a result, the people who work for them are simply not motivated to achieve extraordinary results."

"Precisely!" exclaimed Sam. "But there's more to taming the X-Factor than just *thinking* win-win. Let's go back to the model. Notice there are four parts or steps: Plans, Relationships, Agreements, and Maintenance. It's referred to as the PRAM Model because PRAM is an acronym for the four steps. What I'd like to do now is show you how the PRAM Model works. Then we'll go and visit a couple of my vice presidents and let them show you how they use it to tame the X-Factor and achieve extraordinary results."

"It sounds great to me," said Phil.

CHAPTER

5

Step One: Plans

"The first step in taming the X-Factor is to plan," said Sam. "Extraordinary results don't happen by accident; they happen for a reason."

"That's interesting," responded Phil. "Most of the experts I talked to, as well as the authors whose works I read, agreed that planning is an important part of managing."

"I'm sure they did," replied Sam. "The problem, however, is that when most so-called management experts talk about planning, what they're referring to are things like setting goals, making forecasts, putting together budgets, analyzing data, and looking for new ways to reduce costs. While these activities may have their place in the overall scheme of things, they have very little impact on your achieving extraordinary results as a manager."

"Let me guess," said Phil. "The reason these traditional planning activities do not enable a manager to achieve extraordinary results is that they are not about people."

"Right you are," said Sam. "You're beginning to make some very important connections. If you expect to tame the X-Factor, your plan has to take into account that your success as a manager depends on people and that people are motivated by self-interest."

"Is putting together such a plan difficult?" asked Phil.

"Not really," answered Sam. "Like every other aspect of taming the X-Factor, *the truly difficult part is remembering to do it*. Remember that dictum, Phil: 'The truly difficult part is remembering to do it.'"

Sam then walked over to his flip chart and picked up a marker. "There are basically four steps for putting together a plan to tame the X-Factor. I'll write them down first and then discuss them with you using a couple of examples." It took Sam just a few minutes to write the four steps on the flip chart. When he finished, the chart read:

DEVELOPING A PLAN
TO TAME THE X-FACTOR

1. Determine your self-interest.

2. Identify those people who stand between you and success.

3. Determine their self-interest.

4. Develop a plan to connect the self-interests.

"Let's start with a familiar example to illustrate these four steps," said Sam as he turned to face Phil. "I'd like you to try to put yourself in the shoes of the management of that hotel that succeeded in getting me to reuse my towels. What do you think was the self-interest of the management of that hotel?"

"To lower the hotel's laundering costs by getting guests to reuse some of their towels," responded Phil.

"Good," said Sam. "Who do you think were the people who stood between the management of this hotel and the successful achievement of its self-interest?"

"The hotel guests," replied Phil.

"Right again," said Sam. "Now, what do you think the management of this hotel determined might be an important self-interest of many of the guests?"

"Doing their part, as responsible citizens, to help preserve the environment," answered Phil.

"And what was the plan to connect these self-interests?" asked Sam.

"To put a card on the bathroom counter of each guest room that would inform each guest of an immediate opportunity to pursue his or her self-interest," said Phil.

"There you have it," proclaimed Sam. "You have just put together a plan to tame the X-Factor."

"It's truly amazing how simple this all is, once you realize what's going on," said Phil.

"Yes, it is," responded Sam. "But keep in mind that was a relatively simple example where the hotel's management only wanted its guests to perform a single, simple act that required almost no thought or energy. Now, let's take a look at how the managers at my company utilize these four steps to develop their plans to tame the X-Factor. We'll do this in general terms for now, and we'll get more specific later on when we visit a couple of my vice presidents."

Sam paused, then asked Phil, "In general terms, what do you think is the basic self-interest of every one of my managers?"

"To achieve extraordinary results."

"Exactly," responded Sam. "Now, who stands between these managers and whether they achieve these extraordinary results?"

"The people who work for them."

"So far, so good," said Sam. "Let's see how you do on this next planning step. What do you suppose represents the self-interest of these people?"

Phil hesitated. "I'm really not sure. I hate to admit it, but I'm not sure I know."

"Don't feel bad," said Sam. "Most managers don't have a clue." Sam walked back to the flip chart. As he began to write, he said, "There are three components to people's self-interest a manager has to be concerned with." When he finished, the chart read:

- **RESPECT**
- **MEANING**
- **RENEWAL**

"These three words may not seem all that profound to you at first, but they represent nearly everything people are looking for in their jobs. If you can effectively arrange for each of these three components, you will have succeeded in taming the X-Factor."

Sam continued, "Let's start with respect. What do you suppose respect means to people who work?"

"It means they want to be taken seriously as individuals by their manager," answered Phil.

"Right!" exclaimed Sam. "They don't want to be looked down upon, talked down to, or otherwise treated like children by their manager, nor do they want to feel they are being exploited. Instead, they want to feel that they are in partnership with their manager and that their manager really does care about them."

"Why is respect so important?" asked Phil.

"Would you get excited about going the extra mile for a manager who didn't care about you, but was only out to exploit you?" asked Sam.

"No way!" answered Phil.

"Neither would anyone else," replied Sam.

"That makes a great deal of sense," said Phil. "If a manager doesn't truly respect his or her people, there is no way they'll even consider helping him or her achieve extraordinary results."

"Well put," responded Sam. "Now, let's take a look at the next component of job-related self-interest. What do you think meaning represents to people who work?" asked Sam.

"It probably has something to do with the fact that

people prefer to direct their energies toward something they feel is inherently worthwhile," said Phil.

"Right again!" affirmed Sam, smiling. "You see, people really want more than just jobs, they want to pursue a *cause* they believe in. They want to make a difference. This is what produces the necessary excitement that will enable you to tame the X-Factor. Pursuing a cause is the only thing that will take a loose collection of individuals, each with his or her own personal agenda, and turn it into a cohesive team. It's also what makes work fun."

"So if I want to tame the X-Factor, I must first transform the work at hand into a cause that my people believe in."

"You've got it," said Sam. "This is where the manager shifts gears and assumes the role of a *leader*. You see, leaders create causes that generate excitement and galvanize people."

After a pause Sam suggested, "Let's move on to the third component of job-related self-interest. What do you think renewal is all about?"

"People can't continue to work indefinitely at high levels of effort and excitement without somehow having their batteries recharged," answered Phil.

"That's exactly what renewal is all about," agreed Sam. "You see, paychecks *alone* are not enough to sustain high levels of excitement and effort, because they are not the reason people get excited about what they are doing in the first place. Paychecks are extremely important, but people need something *in addition* to their paychecks to sustain a high level of excitement and effort."

"And what's that?" asked Phil.

"It's really quite simple," replied Sam. "Individuals need to feel that they *and* their contributions to the cause are genuinely appreciated by their manager."

"I can see why this is so important," said Phil. "If your manager doesn't show any appreciation for you and your hard work, the excitement disappears and the idea of working hard quickly loses its appeal, no matter how noble the cause."

"That's it exactly," replied Sam. "Now that you understand the three components of work-related self-interest, it's time to look at the last step in putting together a plan to tame the X-Factor: to develop a plan to connect the self-interest of my managers (to achieve extraordinary results) with the self-interest of the people who work for them (respect, meaning, and renewal)."

"Is developing a plan to connect these self-interests a difficult thing to do?" asked Phil.

"Not at all," replied Sam. "Once you understand the PRAM Model, all the necessary planning is already done for you. All you, as the manager, have to do is commit to executing the remaining three steps of the PRAM Model (Relationships, Agreements, and Maintenance), and the two sets of self-interests will connect *automatically*."

Phil was somewhat puzzled. "I'm not sure I follow," he said.

In response Sam went to the flip chart and started adding to what was written there. When he finished, the chart read:

- RESPECT—RELATIONSHIPS STEP
- MEANING—AGREEMENTS STEP
- RENEWAL—MAINTENANCE STEP

"Let me explain," said Sam. "The Relationships step of the PRAM Model deals with the respect component of job-related self-interest. The reason is that the only way you can develop a personal relationship with the people who work for you is to show a genuine interest in them and demonstrate to them that you care. This is what respect is all about. The Agreements step is all about creating meaning for your people. In this step, you work with your people as partners to transform the work at hand into a cause that both excites and galvanizes them. The Maintenance step of the PRAM Model is all about renewal. This is where you regularly demonstrate to your people that you sincerely appreciate all their hard work and that you continue to respect each of them as individuals."

"There is more to the PRAM Model than I initially imagined," said Phil. "I'm anxious to learn how to execute these next three steps."

"That's what we're going to talk about next," asserted Sam. "We'll start with the Relationships step, move on to the Agreements step, then talk about Maintenance. This is the order in which these three steps *must* be executed if you expect to tame the X-Factor."

"Are you saying that if I can do all the right things, but in the wrong order, I still won't succeed in taming the X-Factor?" asked Phil.

"That's right," confirmed Sam. "On the other hand, if you do the right things in the right order, the results you are looking for are virtually guaranteed."

"So many steps," said Phil, trying hard to conceal his uncertainty.

"Don't worry—they all come together quite naturally," Sam assured him. "Let's move on to the Relationships step of the PRAM Model."

Phil then pulled out a notepad to record what he has just learned.

Plans: A Summary

Developing a Plan to tame the X-Factor is simple. As a manager, you need to:

1. Determine your self-interest, which is achieving extraordinary results.

2. Identify those people who stand between you
   and success.

3. Determine their self-interest.
   a. Respect.
   b. Meaning.
   c. Renewal.

4. Execute the remaining three steps of the
   PRAM Model to connect the two sets of self-
   interests.

Step Two: Relationships

S am walked back over to the flip chart and proceeded to make his next entry. When he finished, the chart read:

TYPES OF BUSINESS RESOURCES

- HUMAN RESOURCES
- NONHUMAN RESOURCES

Sam turned to Phil and said, "This may initially sound trivial, but there are basically two types of resources available to any business. There are *human* resources, which are people, and *nonhuman* resources, which include things like money, machines, and materials. The Relationships step of the PRAM Model is about acknowledging and taking very seriously the fact that human resources are quite different from nonhuman resources. As such, they require a *totally* different method of managing than do nonhuman resources."

"Don't most people in managerial positions already know this?" asked Phil.

"Yes, they do," replied Sam, "but they don't take it seriously. If there is one thing that has stood in the way of any real progress in the field of managing, it is the failure of scholars, experts, and practitioners to take seriously this all-important distinction between human and nonhuman resources. You see, the nonhuman resources of a business—like machines, for example—are dead, inert objects. They don't think; they don't possess emotions, egos, or self-interest; and they don't retaliate when they feel they've been wronged. In addition, they don't need to be motivated in order to perform well, they are willing to work 24 hours a day, and they follow orders without question. Furthermore, they are not concerned with job security, they have no need to be recognized for their accomplishments, and when they are no longer needed they can be discarded without consequences."

"I know a number of managers who would say that this sounds like a description of an ideal employee," chuckled Phil.

"I'll bet you do," replied Sam, "but I'll also bet none of them is a great manager who regularly achieves extraordinary results."

"You're absolutely right on that one," concurred Phil.

Sam went on, "Managing nonhuman resources is really quite simple. All the information necessary to manage these resources is available, quantifiable, measurable, and easily compared to some predetermined standard or goal. I'm talking about things like return on investment, output per hour, reject rate, and so forth. Then, based on an analysis of the results of these comparisons, the manager makes the necessary decisions in a rational or analytical manner from a very detached vantage point."

"Isn't this often referred to as *managing by the numbers?*" asked Phil.

"Exactly," replied Sam, "and it's precisely the way nonhuman resources *should* be managed. On the other hand, managing by the numbers breaks down quickly when it's applied to people."

"Why is that?" asked Phil.

"Because people are very different from nonhuman resources in some very important ways," replied Sam. "First of all, they are *alive*, not inert, which means they can think instead of merely responding. As such, they choose to behave in ways that they deem best serve *their* self-interests. This means they decide how hard they'll work, how well they'll cooperate, and how strongly they'll commit to a set of goals. Furthermore, if they think they've been wronged, they'll retaliate, and if they don't like the system of numbers they're being managed with, they'll devise ingenious ways to beat it. On the other hand, they react very positively to genuine kindness, friendship, and caring. In addition, they work best in an environment where they feel secure, they're taken seriously as individuals, and their efforts are appreciated and recognized—an environment where they feel *respected* as individuals."

"I think I'm starting to see the point," said Phil. "Applying management by the numbers to people takes the human element out of something that by its very nature *has* to be human."

"Exactly!" exclaimed Sam. "You see, managing human resources strictly by the numbers means managers seldom have to interact with their people, which allows them to remain aloof and detached. This puts them in a position where they actually try to manage their people as if they actually *are* non-human resources like machines. The idea behind managing people by the numbers is for managers somehow to develop the right set of performance standards or metrics, put them in place, and then hold their people accountable to achieve those performance standards. Once actual performance occurs, the manager's role is to reward only those who perform at or above the standard—a job rendered much easier because of the manager's detachment from his or her people."

"I've never thought about it this way before," mused Phil, "but managing people by the numbers sends them a very clear message that they, as individuals, are not respected, are expendable, are taken for granted, and are unappreciated."

"Absolutely," replied Sam.

Phil thought for a few seconds and then asked, "If managing people by the numbers sends them the wrong message, then why is it that so many managers use that approach?"

"Excellent question," responded Sam. "There are basically two reasons. First, it's all they know. It's what they were taught in business schools, and it's the method of managing that's reinforced by *their* managers. Second, managing people by the numbers does produce results, although they don't hold a candle to the results associated with taming the X-Factor. You see, most people need money in order to feed their families and pay their bills. So, up to a point, they are willing to let themselves be ordered around and controlled by numbers in exchange for a paycheck. But that's as far as it goes. If you insist on managing people by the numbers, don't even think about achieving extraordinary results."

"If managing by the numbers doesn't work, then how do you manage people if you want to tame the X-Factor?" asked Phil.

Sam looked at Phil and smiled. "What step of the PRAM Model are we talking about right now?"

"Relationships."

"That's right!" exclaimed Sam. "You manage people with a management tool that's 100 percent human—*relationships*."

"I'm not sure I follow," admitted Phil.

"Do you remember how, just a few minutes ago, you said that applying managing by the numbers to human resources took the human element out of something that by its very nature had to be human?" asked Sam.

"Yes, I do," nodded Phil.

Sam went on, "Well, managing through relationships puts the necessary humanity back into the process of managing people. You see, before you can manage through relationships, you first have to *develop* relationships. And that will force you to do something very human that managing by the numbers does not. It forces you to get out of your office and become personally involved with each of your people, because personal involvement is the only way that relationships can be developed."

"What does this personal involvement entail?" asked Phil.

"Lots of informal contact," responded Sam. "For example, each manager of this company regularly and frequently circulates among his or her people soliciting their thoughts and opinions while actively listening to what they have to say. Listening is key because it sends a very clear message that the manager really does believe that each individual is important."

"Isn't this what Hewlett-Packard refers to as Managing By Wandering Around, or MBWA?" asked Phil.

"Exactly!" exclaimed Sam. "And just like Hewlett-Packard, we embrace this activity as an extremely important part of our company's culture and view it as a key component to our tremendous overall success!"

"I hear what you are saying, but I'm still not exactly sure why relationships are so important," said Phil.

Sam explained, "You see, relationships, as they develop, naturally lead to the one thing that is absolutely necessary if you expect to tame the X-Factor."

"What's that?" asked Phil.

Sam walked back over to his flip chart and wrote a single word in large letters. The chart read:

```
TRUST
```

Phil contemplated what was written on the flip chart. "This is very interesting," he said. "I've seen the notion of trust tossed around in numerous publications recently, but none of the authors seemed really to know what to do with it or where it fits in the overall scheme of things."

"Excellent observation!" exclaimed Sam. "Let me show you where it fits in. You see, people are very willing to go the extra mile for a manager they trust, but they won't even consider doing so for a manager they don't trust."

"I agree," said Phil.

Sam continued, "When the trust level is high, people feel confident that the situation between them and their manager is going to be win-win. That is, if they go the extra mile for their manager, they know that their manager is going to reciprocate in some meaningful way. This is what trust is all about. On the other hand, if there is no trust, people automatically assume the situation between them and their manager is going to be win-lose. That is, if they go the extra mile for their manager, they will simply be taken advantage of."

"This goes back to the issue of self-interest, doesn't it?"

"You bet," replied Sam. "When the trust level is high, people see very clearly that working hard to help their manager pursue his or her self-interest (extraordinary results) is also the vigorous pursuit of their own. In other words, they *know* the manager isn't going to take advantage of them. As a result, they can become highly motivated to direct their best efforts toward this pursuit. On the other hand, if there is no trust, people don't see any connection between helping their manager pursue his or her self-interest and the pursuit of their own. Without this connection, there is absolutely no reason for them to get excited about helping their manager achieve extraordinary results, so they don't."

"What this means," said Phil, "is that if there is no trust between me and the people who work for me, the best I can expect is that these people will do what they have to in order to keep collecting their paychecks—and little more."

"Right you are," agreed Sam. "Furthermore, since most managers don't understand this all-important role that trust plays in their achieving extraordinary results, they don't spend any time intentionally developing it with their people. This, as much as any single factor, helps explain why so many managers achieve ordinary results."

"Well—" Phil paused. "—I agree that trust is a critical ingredient of a manager's success, but how do I go about the business of developing it with the people who work for me?"

"It's really quite simple," said Sam. "First of all, keep in mind what trust is. It's the mutual assurance of knowing that if I go the extra mile for you, when it's your turn you are going to go the extra mile for me. Second, realize that trust is something that has to be earned through action. You can't convince people with an argument that it's in their best interest to trust you. If you could, the least trusted phrase in the English language wouldn't be 'Trust me.'"

Phil chuckled.

Sam continued, "Third, recognize, as I said earlier, that relationships, as they develop, naturally lead to trust. If you practice Managing By Wandering Around, you have a system for building relationships already in place. As you regularly visit with the people who work for you, look for opportunities to demonstrate that you genuinely care about them and you take very seriously the fact that your most important job as a manager is to support them."

"How do I go about doing that?" asked Phil.

Sam smiled. "While it may sound trivial, the most important thing you do to demonstrate that you care about the people who work for you is to ask for their thoughts and opinions, listen to what they have to say, and then take whatever constructive action is required. The key that really makes this work is always to be yourself. You see, managers who achieve extraordinary results are not arrogant or superficial, they don't play games, and they are not powermongers. Instead, they are *real*, and that's how they come across to their people."

"It sounds like the managers at your company really do take seriously the fact that people are their most important resource," remarked Phil.

"Absolutely," responded Sam, "and the culture at this company strongly supports that practice. In addition to Managing By Wandering Around, every manager at this company, including me, practices an open-door policy. These two activities provide numerous opportunities for managers to build relationships that eventually lead to trust."

"What you are saying is that you have created a culture at this company that makes a manager's job of building relationships both easy and natural," said Phil.

"Right you are—and our commitment to informality makes that job even easier. For example, everyone at this company is on a first-name basis. Every manager, including me, works out of a wall-less, doorless office, and there are no heady titles that connote one person is more important than another. Furthermore, information about this company and how it is doing is not hoarded by managers as a source of power, but rather it is openly shared with everyone."

"I'm very impressed," said Phil. "I have never heard of a company culture that so directly facilitated a manager's doing the right things."

"I'll take that as a compliment," said Sam with a smile. "But it's really not all that difficult once you understand what the right things are."

"There's one thing that still puzzles me," said Phil.

"What's that?"

"Respect," replied Phil. "We haven't talked about the respect component of job-related self-interest. Isn't that what the Relationships step of the PRAM Model is supposed to be all about?"

"It is," responded Sam, smiling. "When you, as a

manager, take the time to do all the necessary things to develop relationships that lead to trust with each of the people who work for you, you have clearly demonstrated that you respect them."

"So building relationships that lead to trust and showing respect are the same thing?" asked Phil.

"They sure are," said Sam. "Once your people feel that you respect them as individuals, you are now in a position to get them excited about what they are doing—which leads us to the Agreements step of the PRAM Model.

Once again, Phil pulled out his notepad to record what he had just learned.

Relationships: A Summary

Before people can get excited about helping their manager achieve extraordinary results, they must first feel that their manager respects them as individuals. Showing respect is easy. As a manager, you need to build Relationships with your people that lead to trust. You do this by:

1. Regularly and frequently circulating among your people.

2. Asking for their thoughts and opinions.

3. Listening to what they have to say.

4. Taking whatever constructive action is required.

Step Three: Agreements

Once again, Sam walked over to his flip chart. This time he wrote:

BASIC JOB DIMENSIONS

- WHAT
- WHY

"There are two basic dimensions to every job," said Sam. "There's the *what* dimension and the *why* dimension. What do you suppose the 'what' dimension is all about?"

"Probably the basic content and nature of the job," Phil responded. "This would include things like the variety of tasks to be performed, the level of challenge and effort associated with these tasks, the amount of autonomy given to the individual who is performing these tasks, as well as the performance expectations and the pay associated with the job."

"That's it exactly," said Sam. "The way in which these elements of the 'what' dimension are structured is what makes a job more or less pleasant, attractive, or satisfying. The problem, however, is that the 'what' dimension of a job, no matter how carefully it is configured, cannot get people excited about going the extra mile to help their manager accomplish extraordinary results."

"I wonder why that is," mused Phil.

"Because performing a series of tasks in exchange for a paycheck, *by itself*, does not provide the individual with any sense of meaning," explained Sam. "You see, performing a job only for a paycheck is like walking on a treadmill. Once you realize that your effort is taking you nowhere, the job quickly loses its appeal and becomes boring."

"What I hear you saying," said Phil, "is that when jobs *do* provide individuals with a sense of meaning, they don't see themselves on a treadmill. Instead, they see themselves in pursuit of a worthy cause or goal that they believe in."

"Absolutely," said Sam. "It's the pursuit of such a cause that creates the excitement necessary to tame the X-Factor. This is what the 'why' dimension of a job is all about."

"I hear what you are saying," said Phil, "but I'm not totally sure I understand where the excitement comes from."

"Let me share something with you that happened to me a long time ago," said Sam. "When I was in high school, I played two different years on varsity basketball teams. One year, I started every game and was the team's leading scorer. The next year, I mostly sat on the bench and was used as a practice player. Which experience do you think I found most exciting?"

"Obviously, playing for the team where you started every game and were the team's leading scorer," answered Phil.

"What makes you think that?" asked Sam.

"You were the star," declared Phil. "You were the person who got all the press clippings."

Sam smiled. "Now let me tell you the rest of the story. The year I started every game and was the leading scorer, the team did not win one game all season. But the year I sat on the bench most of the time, the team won the state championship. Now which experience do you think I found most exciting?"

Phil looked at Sam, shook his head, and smiled because he knew Sam had just set him up. "The one where the team won the state championship," he answered.

"You bet," said Sam. "And why do you suppose that was the case?"

"Because," answered Phil, "even as the star player, you were part of a losing cause. You may have racked up lots of individual statistics, but all that effort took you nowhere. I'll bet losing probably became very frustrating and embarrassing after a while."

"Quite frankly," said Sam, "I thought the season would never end. I actually considered quitting the team on several occasions."

Phil continued, "On the other team, you may have sat on the bench and been mainly used as a practice player, but your efforts were directed toward a cause that had meaning—winning a state championship. That entire experience must have made you feel really great."

"The memory of that championship season still excites me today," said Sam.

"I think I'm starting to understand the connection between meaning and excitement," said Phil. "What I'd really like to know is what was it that made the difference between those two teams?"

"It was the coach," replied Sam. "The person who coached the team that lost all its games knew his basketball well and was a real taskmaster during practice. The problem was, he never took the time to help us set some team goals. He just told us to go out there and win. With no cause to rally around, we really never came together as a team. As a result, each team member basically looked out for himself by trying to pad his own personal statistics. And the more we lost, the worse the situation became, because individual statistics were the only thing left to play for. The whole experience was very negative."

"What happened the next year?" asked Phil. "Did you get a new coach?"

"We did," said Sam. "Our new coach wasn't as knowledgeable about the game of basketball, and he wasn't nearly the taskmaster during practice, but he definitely understood what a sense of meaning or purpose could do for a basketball team."

"What did he do that was different?" asked Phil.

"After he made a thorough assessment of the talent on our team, he came to us with a plan. He told us that he had decided to go with a smaller, faster starting lineup rather than the taller, slower starting lineup we had the previous year. He felt our speed was our competitive edge. He acknowledged that some of us wouldn't see as much playing time as the previous year, while others would see a lot more."

"How did his plan affect you?" asked Phil.

"I admit," said Sam, "that as one of the taller but slower starters, I didn't like his plan one bit. I remember standing there in the locker room with my arms folded across my chest."

"So what happened?" asked Phil.

"What the coach said next caught us all by sur-prise," said Sam. "He said, given the talent we had, if we all pulled together as a team and worked hard, he thought a state championship was within reach."

"At this point, I'll bet your new coach had every player's attention," said Phil.

"You bet he did," responded Sam. "Winning a state championship was something every one of us had secretly fantasized about, but thought could never happen. Now here was our new coach telling us that if we accepted our roles and worked hard, our wildest dream could become a reality. From that day forward, we were on a mission. We were no longer a loose collection of individuals who got to-gether to play basketball. Instead, we were a highly committed team in pursuit of a dream. We were all very excited."

"Did pursuing the goal of a state championship change your attitude toward your role as a bench-warmer and practice player?" asked Phil.

"Absolutely," responded Sam. "You see, pursuing the dream of a state championship gave meaning to the role of being a practice or reserve player. Our jobs were every bit as important as those who were in the starting lineup. The better job we did as prac-tice players, the better we prepared our starting team for the next game. Also, as reserves, we had to be ready to step in and play in the event the person playing in front of us got into foul trouble or became injured. Let me tell you, our practices were intense and everyone worked hard."

"What an amazing story," remarked Phil. "It certainly clarifies the connection between meaning and excitement. But what is it about meaning that creates the excitement?"

"That's a very good question," said Sam. "Most people don't realize it, but the most dominant and pressing need among human beings is to find meaning in their lives. People want to make a contribution toward something that matters and know that their life stands for something that's good. So powerful is this need that humans are in a constant, persistent, almost desperate search for it."

"I see where the excitement comes from," said Phil. "Since people are almost desperate in their search for meaning, when they do find it, they become ecstatic."

"Do they ever," responded Sam. "What's more, once people find a sense of meaning in their lives, they are more than willing to work very hard, doing whatever it takes, in order to hang on to it."

"It's all starting to fall into place," said Phil, "and it seems so simple. All managers need to do in order to get people excited about going the extra mile to help them accomplish extraordinary results is somehow to connect their ever-present and dominant need for meaning to the work that needs to be done."

"That's it," said Sam with a smile. "It's really easy

when you think about it. The need for meaning is already there, and people are almost desperate to fulfill it. All you have to do is provide people with an opportunity to find meaning in what they do, and all of a sudden you have ordinary people accomplishing extraordinary results."

"If this is so simple and works so well, why don't more people manage this way?" asked Phil.

"Excellent question," responded Sam. "The ironic thing about the need for meaning is that while it is humans' most dominant and pressing need, most people are seldom aware that they are seeking it. It's something you just don't think about all that much. Because of this, the need for meaning has received very little attention from management scholars and even less attention from management practitioners."

"Do you know what I find even more ironic?" asked Phil.

"What's that?"

"That the most powerful motivator is such a well-kept secret."

"Good point," said Sam, "and one that helps explain why there aren't more great managers. If a manager isn't aware of the most powerful motivator, it's impossible for that manager to tame the X-Factor."

"Is connecting people's need for meaning with the work to be done a difficult thing to do?" asked

Phil. "Doesn't meaning mean different things to different people?"

"There's good news and bad news," replied Sam with a smile. "The bad news is meaning does mean different things to different people. The good news is that, at work, there is one thing that seems to be universal in its appeal to satisfy people's need for meaning."

"What's that?" asked Phil.

Sam walked over to his flip chart and wrote:

BEING THE BEST

"If you observe different companies that are truly the leaders in their respective fields, you'll find that they all have one thing in common: They are committed to being the best at something. You see," continued Sam, "one of the most fundamental aspects of meaning is that people prefer to think of themselves as winners rather than losers. As a result, they are constantly searching for ways to validate this idea. One way for people to validate themselves as winners is to be part of an organization that is either the best at what it does or is committed to becoming the best."

"This makes so much sense," said Phil. "Being part of an organization that is committed to being the best provides an individual with very convincing validation that he or she is, in fact, a winner."

"Right on," replied Sam. "Being part of something that's the best creates excitement and extraordinary effort from the top of an organization all the way down to the trenches. Ask any employees at Intel who the world's largest chip maker is, and they are only too happy to tell you. Ask employees of Southwest Airlines which airline is the best, and they'll proudly tell you that Southwest is the number one airline in terms of on-time performance, baggage handling, and customer satisfaction. You'll find the same holds true at Nordstrom, Disney, Ritz-Carlton, and Hewlett-Packard. Each of the companies is a leader in its respective field, and each is the very best at what it does."

"Very impressive," said Phil. "But how do I, as a manager, figure out what to be the best at?"

"It's all very simple: You ask the people who work for you to help you figure this out."

"And how do I go about doing that?"

"You bring your people together for a series of meetings and ask them to help you answer three questions." Sam then walked over to his flip chart and began to write. When he finished, the chart read:

- WHAT THINGS DO WE WANT TO BECOME THE <u>BEST</u> AT?
- HOW DO WE DEFINE <u>BEST</u>?
- HOW DO WE GO ABOUT BECOMING THE <u>BEST</u> AT THE THINGS WE'VE CHOSEN?

Sam continued, "Depending on the size of your organization, this process may take a few meetings, but a consensus will eventually emerge for each of these questions. At this point, you will have successfully connected the need for meaning in the people who work for you with the work to be done. You will have transformed the work to be done into a cause that your people are excited about. Now, instead of having a loose collection of individuals, all with their own agendas, you have a highly cohesive team that is committed to working very hard to help you, their manager, accomplish extraordinary results."

"I think going through this process could be very exciting," declared Phil.

"It is," replied Sam, "and, what's more, it's fun. It is also an excellent opportunity to reinforce the fact that you respect the people who work for you; that is, you really do take each of them seriously as an individual."

"I think I understand the meaning component of work-related self-interest. But this was also supposed to be a discussion about the Agreements step of the PRAM Model. So far, we haven't even mentioned the word 'agreement.' How does the concept of an agreement fit into all this?" asked Phil.

"What would you call the process of getting your people excited about going the extra mile to help you accomplish extraordinary results in exchange for your providing them with an opportunity to fulfill their need for meaning?" asked Sam.

Phil shook his head, looked over at Sam, smiled, and said, "You've got me again. That is the process of reaching an agreement between a manager and his or her people."

"Amen," said Sam with a chuckle, "and a win-win one at that! Now, let's talk about the Maintenance step of the PRAM Model."

At this point, Phil pulled out his notepad and proceeded to make his next entry.

Agreements: A Summary

Meaning is what creates the excitement necessary to tame the X-Factor. Creating opportunities for people to satisfy their need for meaning at work is easy. As a manager, you need to reach an Agreement with your people concerning:

1. What things do we want to become the *best* at?
2. How to we define *best*?
3. How do we go about becoming the *best* at the things we've chosen?

CHAPTER
8

Step Four: Maintenance

S am walked over to his desk and picked up a windup toy mouse, turned the key several times, and set the mouse on the floor. The mouse immediately took off in a rapidly changing zigzag circular pattern. After about 10 seconds it stopped.

"Why did the mouse stop?" asked Sam.

"Because the spring that propelled the mouse ran down," answered Phil.

"That's right," said Sam. "Now, can you think of any way to prevent this from happening?"

"Yes," answered Phil. "All you need to do is figure out some way to wind the spring back up at the same time it is winding down."

"Exactly!" exclaimed Sam. "Because the energy source propelling the mouse would then be in a constant state of renewal, meaning the mouse could go on indefinitely. This same thing holds true for the people who work for you. At this point in the process, you've got these people excited, and their excitement is like the spring that is inside the toy mouse. It is the energy source that enables them to go the extra mile to help you, their manager, achieve extraordinary results. If you expect to become a great manager, you've got to keep this excitement level from winding down. This is what the renewal component of work-related self-interest and the Maintenance step of the PRAM Model are all about."

"What I hear you saying," said Phil, "is that if I expect to become a great manager, it's up to me to keep the excitement level of the people who work for me in a constant state of renewal."

"Precisely!" exclaimed Sam. "As long as they remain excited, they will continue to go the extra mile, which means you'll continue to accomplish extraordinary results as a manager. On the other hand, the minute the excitement runs down, you go right back to being a good manager who achieves ordinary results."

"It seems a bit overwhelming to think of being

able to sustain a high level of excitement over the long term," reflected Phil.

"Not at all. The concept of renewal is all about demonstrating, in *several* very important ways, that you really do respect and care about the people who work for you. In fact, it's the easiest and most fun part of taming the X-Factor. All you need to do is maintain the three things you already have in place."

Sam once again walked over to his trusty flip chart and began to write. When he finished, the chart read:

RENEWAL MEANS YOU MUST MAINTAIN

- **YOUR AGREEMENTS**
- **YOUR RELATIONSHIPS**
- **YOUR PLANS**

"I see why this step of the PRAM Model is called Maintenance," said Phil, "but are you also telling me that renewal has *three* separate and distinct dimensions?"

"Yes, and if you expect to tame the X-Factor, you have to deal with all three of them effectively."

"How do I do all this?" asked Phil.

"Let's start at the top of the list with agreements. You made an agreement with your people to provide them with an opportunity to satisfy their need for meaning in exchange for their getting excited about going the extra mile to help you achieve extraordinary results. One very important aspect of keeping this excitement alive is to make sure that you hold up your end of the agreement."

"How do I accomplish this?" asked Phil.

Sam smiled. "When you put together this agreement with your people, you either implicitly or explicitly promised them two things."

Once again Sam walked over to his flip chart and began to write. When he finished, the chart read:

- **SUPPORT**
- **VALIDATION AS WINNERS**

"Support," said Sam, "means that you, as a manager, have to *walk the talk* when it comes to living out your commitment to your people—that is, that you do, in fact, take seriously the idea that they are your most important resource and that your number one job is to *support* them."

"How do I do this?"

"By providing your people with the tools, training, resources, and freedom necessary to enable them to do their jobs well. You see, the pursuit of even the most noble cause quickly loses its excitement if you don't receive the support you need to do your job well. It's like being asked to paint a large house with a small paintbrush when you know that a paint sprayer is available that would enable you to do this job much faster and better, but your manager won't let you use it."

"This makes sense," said Phil. "Not receiving the support necessary to do your job well is almost like being on a treadmill. You expend a large amount of energy but make very little progress toward the end you are trying to achieve. This can be very frustrating."

riding a stationary bicycle

"Absolutely," responded Sam. "And once this frustration occurs, the excitement disappears, which means there is no way that you are going to achieve extraordinary results."

"I think I see another problem," said Phil.

"What's that?" asked Sam.

"By not providing this necessary support, you are sending your people a very clear message that you are not really committed to the cause. This, in turn, undermines the trust between you and your people—which diminishes your effectiveness as a manager even further."

"Excellent point!" exclaimed Sam.

He paused to reflect for a few seconds and then continued. "The second aspect of maintaining your agreement with your people is validating each of them as a winner. Let's assume now that your people have performed the way you wanted them to. They have gone the extra mile to help you accomplish extraordinary results. What this means is that your people have expended a great amount of energy over a sustained period of time, and now you look like a hero, right? If you expect them to continue this high level of performance on your behalf, then you have to make it worth their while."

"How do I do this?" asked Phil.

"Remember how earlier in our discussion I pointed out that win-win is at the heart of taming the X-Factor?"

"Yes, I do," said Phil.

"Well," continued Sam, "because of the hard work of your people, you look like a superstar as a manager—that's your win. Now it's up to you to make sure that all the hard work they have expended on your behalf also results in a win for them. What you want to avoid here is what I call the Vietnam War syndrome."

"Vietnam War syndrome?" said Phil with a perplexed look on his face.

Sam smiled and continued. "I, like many other people, spent some time in the Army during the Vietnam War. During my tour of duty, I spent a year in Vietnam. Before I went over there, the Army trained me very well and got me very excited about the noble causes of serving my country and doing my part to help preserve freedom. When I arrived in Vietnam, the Army provided me with the best equipment in the world to enable me to do my job. In other words, the Army *supported* me very well. For the next 12 months, I worked 12 or more hours a day, seven days a week, with only one week off for rest and recuperation."

"Wasn't it hot and very humid over there, too?" interjected Phil.

"You bet it was," said Sam. "I worked very hard that year in a hostile environment, all the while thinking I was doing a good thing. During that time spent in a combat zone, I literally risked my life to pursue what I assumed to be a noble cause on behalf of my country. When I returned home, I was very proud of what I had done and I was quite surprised when I found out that nobody back here appreciated it. There was no welcoming committee, no parade, no celebration—not even a genuine 'thank you' from anyone."

"I'll bet you were devastated," said Phil.

"Devastated, depressed, and very angry," responded Sam. "Here I had just gone the extra mile, even risked my life, and all I was going to get in return were paychecks and some educational benefits."

"That doesn't sound like win-win to me," said Phil. "You must have felt betrayed and taken advantage of."

"I sure did," replied Sam. "As a result, instead of feeling like a winner because of what I had done, I now felt like a loser. Once all this had sunk in, I remember thinking to myself, that if I had a chance to do it again, I'd probably avoid the opportunity altogether by going to Canada until the war was over."

"I'll bet you would have felt just the opposite had you received a hero's welcome when you returned," said Phil.

"You're absolutely right," responded Sam. "Let's go back to my high school days when my team won the state championship. Yes, winning the championship was a wonderful experience in and of itself. But, what made that experience really great were the things that happened afterward. First, when we returned home we were honored with a parade, which was followed by a community-wide assembly where the mayor presented us with keys to the city. Next, there were several television appearances, a visit to the governor's office, and an almost endless string of banquets where we were honored for being the state champions. This whole experience felt so great that I actually regretted not having another year of high school left so that I could take part in pursuing another state championship."

"I had no idea that making people feel great about their accomplishments was so important when it came to sustaining excitement," said Phil. "I would have thought the accomplishments associated with pursuing a meaningful cause such as becoming the best would have been enough by themselves."

"That would be like winning a state championship and having nobody care," said Sam with a smile. "You see, pursuing a cause *creates* the excitement necessary to orchestrate the X-Factor. Feeling really great as a result of these accomplishments validates people as winners and thus *sustains* this excitement."

"Is this where I, the manager, take the time to say 'thank you' personally to my people for all their hard work and accomplishments?" asked Phil.

"Not if you expect to tame the X-Factor," responded Sam.

"I'm not sure I follow," said Phil.

Sam continued, "Your people have just gone the extra mile to help you achieve extraordinary results. At this point they are very proud and excited about their accomplishments, just like my high school basketball team was when we won the state championship. If you, as the manager, expect to sustain this excitement, you can't just *tell* them that you appreciate all their hard work and accomplishments; you have to *show* them, just like the community did after my team won that state championship. The name of the game here is for you, the manager, to make your people feel so great about having gone the extra mile on your behalf that they can't wait for a chance to do it again."

"I see how this makes for a win-win situation," said Phil. "My people have just gone the extra mile to help me accomplish extraordinary results—that's *my* win. When I reciprocate by going the extra mile to make sure they feel great for having done so, thus validating them as winners, that's *their* win."

"That's it exactly," responded Sam. "And this is something that *great* managers do exceptionally well."

"Is there any particular secret that the great managers utilize to make their people feel great after they've accomplished extraordinary results?" asked Phil.

"Absolutely!" exclaimed Sam as he once again walked over to his flip chart. He wrote:

CELEBRATION

"Celebration," said Sam. "Great managers who regularly achieve extraordinary results view celebrating people for their accomplishments as their most powerful management activity."

"What is it about celebrating that makes it so powerful?" asked Phil.

"Celebrating the hard work and accomplishments of your people provides convincing validation that they are winners. Doing so renews the human spirit in each of your people and thus recharges their batteries. As a result, your people are once again excited about going the extra mile to help you accomplish the next round of extraordinary results."

"Wait a minute," said Phil. "Celebration was the big difference between your Vietnam experience and your state championship experience."

"It sounds to me like you are beginning to understand why great managers consider celebrating such a powerful management activity," said Sam.

"Yes, I am," said Phil, "but now I have a question for you."

"Let's hear it," responded Sam.

"With celebrating being such an important aspect of sustaining people's excitement, are there any rules concerning how to do it right."

"As a matter of fact, there are," replied Sam. "But don't worry—they are very basic, so they are not at all difficult to follow. First, celebrations have to be real. They cannot come across as simply another superficial gimmick to manipulate your people."

"What you are saying is that to be effective, these

celebrations have to come across as a genuine 'thank you' straight from the manager's heart."

"I couldn't have put it better," said Sam. "The second rule for celebrating is to make sure that you give *all* the credit for the results that have been accomplished to your people. Never try to claim any of it for yourself. Remember, the purpose of these celebrations is to honor your people, not you, for what they've accomplished. Your people have worked hard, they've paid the price, and they've accomplished extraordinary results. Therefore, they deserve all the credit."

"Let me make sure I understand this," said Phil. "This has to do with trust, doesn't it? If you, as the manager, try to take credit for something that your people have worked very hard to achieve, you run a serious risk of violating the trust between you and your people—which would greatly diminish your effectiveness as a manager."

"That's it exactly," said Sam. "Now let's look at the third rule for celebrating. These celebrations must make your people feel really great about what they have achieved. Your people have worked extremely hard, and they are very proud of their accomplishments. Therefore, it's very important that these celebrations provide your people with the opportunity to *revel* in those accomplishments."

"Revel in their accomplishments?" sighed Phil.

"You bet," replied Sam. "And there are lots of things you can do to facilitate that. For example, you can put together a video program and a collage of photographs that enable your people to vividly recall important memories of the journey they undertook to accomplish their extraordinary results. You want your people to recall the excitement and highlights of this journey as well as the hardships they endured and the setbacks they overcame. Probably one of the more important things you could do would be to get someone from senior management, preferably your president, to participate in the celebration. Visual appreciation from the top of the organization adds a lot of excitement to the celebration. You can also contact your communications department and get a group photograph of your people published in the company paper along with an article that praises them for their achievements. You can write personal letters to their families telling them how they should be very proud of their family member who works for you because of the extraordinary accomplishments he or she participated in achieving. As you can see, the things that you can do as a manager to facilitate revelry are limited only by your imagination."

"Tell me, are there any additional rules for making sure you do celebration right?" asked Phil.

"Just one more," replied Sam. "These celebrations have to be fun and festive. It's very important that they come across as play, rather than work. This is where you break out the food, beverages, balloons, banners, music, costumes, games,

contests, or whatever it takes to make the celebration a truly joyous and memorable event. Again,
you are limited only by your imagination."

After a pause, Sam continued. "Now that you understand how to maintain your agreements, let's
look at maintaining your relationships. If you fail to
maintain your relationships with your people, it
doesn't take too long before these relationships begin to deteriorate. Once these relationships deteriorate, the trust that you worked so hard to build
disappears, and the best you can hope for, as a manager, is to achieve ordinary results."

"What you are saying is that maintaining your relationships is every bit as critical for taming the X-
Factor as maintaining your agreements," said Phil.

"Absolutely," responded Sam.

"Is maintaining these relationships a difficult
thing to do?" asked Phil.

"Not really," replied Sam. "The only truly difficult thing about it is remembering to do it, because
it's very easy to overlook. First, continue to do those
things that you did to build those relationships in
the first place."

"Like Managing By Wandering Around?" asked
Phil.

"Exactly," said Sam.

"Is there anything else I can do to maintain these
relationships?" asked Phil.

Sam smiled as he walked back over to his flip

chart. "As a matter of fact, there is," he said as he began to write. Soon the chart read:

```
CELEBRATION
```

"I thought celebration was part of maintaining agreements," said Phil.

"It is," responded Sam with a chuckle, "but that involved celebrating people for their accomplishments. Celebration also has its place when it comes to maintaining relationships where we celebrate people for who they are."

"What sorts of things do you celebrate as part of maintaining relationships?" asked Phil.

"Birthdays, holidays, wedding anniversaries, employment anniversaries, a promotion, the arrival of a new child or grandchild, just to name a few. The idea is for you to use these special occasions as opportunities to bring your people together and have some fun. Obviously, these celebrations are going to be more spontaneous and less elaborate than those associated with maintaining agreements, but they are very important nonetheless. You see, each time you pull your people together to celebrate one of these special occasions, it provides you with an additional opportunity to maintain your relationships with your people. These celebrations also provide opportunities for your people to maintain their relationships with each other, and that's equally important."

"Now all I need to know to tame the X-Factor is how to maintain my plans," said Phil.

"That's right," said Sam. "I think you're going to find this final step interesting because it's unlike anything you've ever heard before. First, let's take a few moments and reflect on your initial plan to tame the X-Factor. Do you remember what your self-interest was?"

"Yes," said Phil. "It was to achieve extraordinary results."

"Do you also remember who the people were who stood between you and success or failure?" asked Sam.

"The people who work for me," answered Phil.

"And what did you determine was their self-interest?" asked Sam.

"The three components of work-related self-interest," answered Phil, "respect, meaning, and renewal."

"How did you plan to connect these two sets of self-interest?" asked Sam.

"To implement the remaining three steps of the

PRAM Model," answered Phil. "Respect is the result of building relationships with my people that lead to trust. Meaning comes from working with my people to transform the work to be done into a cause, namely being the best at something. Renewal would result from providing my people with the support to do their jobs well, validating them as winners, and doing the necessary things to keep my relationships from deteriorating."

"So far, so good. All the management activities that you mentioned in your plan are right on the money. But there is still one very critical managerial activity that stands between you and your being able to tame the X-Factor."

"What's that?"

"You have to figure out some way to *remind* yourself to do these things on a continual and consistent basis," replied Sam.

"Why do I need to do that?"

"Because none of the activities that you mentioned in your plan to tame the X-Factor are reflex managerial behaviors. In other words, you cannot assume that just because you understand all the things that are necessary to tame the X-Factor you are *automatically* going to engage in the correct behavior whenever the situation calls for it. It would be wonderful if that's the way things worked, but they don't. The only way you can make sure that you consistently engage in these behaviors is continually to remind yourself to do so."

"Why is that?"

"It goes back to human nature," replied Sam. "As we discussed earlier, all human beings come into the world already 'programmed,' if you will, to satisfy their basic human needs. This means that pursuing the satisfaction of these needs is not something you have to stop and think about before you do it. Rather, it's an automatic response to the activities and events that are going on in your life. Most of the time people are not even aware that they are pursuing satisfaction of these needs.

"On the other hand, the managerial activities that are necessary for taming the X-Factor involve looking after the needs of others, which is not something we're programmed to do. These behaviors are not automatic behaviors. You have to think about them first before you do them. If you do not continually remind yourself to do those things necessary for taming the X-Factor, you will automatically slip into a behavior pattern that is more consistent with the way you are programmed. As a result, you will gradually become more and more preoccupied with yourself and less and less concerned about your people. You'll do less wandering around, less listening, and less responding, and you'll slowly begin to close your open door. Pretty soon you'll find yourself entertaining thoughts like 'People issues take up too much of my time' or 'My job would be a lot easier if it weren't for the people.' Before you know it, you're back to being an okay manager who gets ordinary results."

"What you've just told me is very sobering," said Phil. "A manager can know all the answers about how to tame the X-Factor and have the best of intentions for doing all of these things, and that still doesn't guarantee he or she will succeed."

"That's right," replied Sam. "Knowledge and good intentions are not enough. You still have to *do* those very things we've been talking about in order to tame the X-Factor. And the only way to guarantee that you'll actually do these things is continually to remind yourself to do them. Let me give you an example. Several years ago, I had the pleasure of visiting the number one Buick dealer in the country in terms of his Customer Service Index score. After we spent a few minutes getting to know each other, I asked him, 'What do you do that makes your dealership so great in terms of customer service?'

"His response was, 'We don't do anything that any other dealerships couldn't do if they wanted to. The only difference is, *we do it!*'

"I responded by saying something like 'That's just great,' as I tried to change the subject.

"At this point, the dealer said to me, 'Just a minute. I can tell you don't get it!'

" 'What don't I get?' I asked.

"He went on to say, 'Every single one of my employees knows that the customer is king and that service is our number one priority. They have all received numerous hours of training on how to give outstanding customer service. If you want to ask any of my employees questions about customer service, you'd quickly find out that they know all the answers. If you gave each one of my employees a lie detector test and asked if they were doing all those things that are necessary to provide outstanding customer service, I guarantee they would all pass with flying colors.'

"I remember commenting at this point, 'I see now why your Customer Service Index score is the best in the country.'

" 'I can see you still don't get it,' he said. 'All I have told you so far is that my people know what to do in order to provide outstanding customer service and that they have good intentions when it comes to doing those things. That, by itself, will not result in the highest Customer Service Index score in the nation.'

" 'What does?' I asked.

" 'Making sure my employees actually do those things that are necessary to provide outstanding customer service. Even though my employees are well trained and have very good intentions, I still have to meet with each one of my departments a minimum of once a week to remind them to do these things. If I don't remind my employees at least once a week, without even realizing it they start to drift into a behavior pattern where they do more and more of the things that please themselves and less and less of the things that please our customers. As a result, our Customer Service Index score will begin to slip. What's even more interesting is that while this is going on, these same people could pass a lie detector test that says they are actually doing all the necessary things to provide outstanding customer service because they truly believe they still are!' "

"That's an amazing story," said Phil. "What it says to me is that if I expect to tame the X-Factor, then I have to remind myself regularly to do those things that enable that to happen, just like that Buick dealer."

"Exactly!" exclaimed Sam. "But when it comes to taming the X-Factor, a once-a-week reminder is not nearly enough."

"How often should I remind myself, and how should I remind myself?" inquired Phil.

"At this company," said Sam, "I ask my managers to ask themselves a question a minimum of three times during the day."

"What is the question?"

Once again Sam walked over to his flip chart and began to write. When he finished, the chart read:

**AM I BEHAVING
LIKE A GREAT
MANAGER?**

You see," explained Sam, "great managers consistently do those things that are necessary to tame the X-Factor. I have found that the best times during the day to answer this question are when you first come to work, right after lunch, and right before you go home. If you can discipline yourself to do this, you'll find that it really does keep you on course. We've also employed a number of visual reminders. Take a quick look around my office and see if you can spot any of them."

Phil took a few seconds to look around Sam's office. "Well," he said, "you have a poster of the PRAM Model on your wall."

"You'll find those hanging all over this company," said Sam. "Do you notice any other visual reminders?"

"I see you have the PRAM Model on your name badge," said Phil.

"That's right," said Sam, "and we also have it on our business cards. Keep looking."

"The screen saver on your computer monitor is a PRAM Model, and you're wearing a pin shaped like an X on your lapel," said Phil.

Sam smiled and said, "Believe me, you can't have too many reminders around that prompt you to do the right things. I also have daily meetings with my managers where we reinforce in each other what taming the X-Factor is all about. We refer to these meetings as X-Meetings. In fact, I just came from one right before I met you."

"Do other companies do this?" asked Phil.

"Ones that are highly successful on a continual basis do," replied Sam. "Take Ritz-Carlton Hotels. This is the only hotel chain to win the Malcolm Baldrige National Quality Award. Every day, each location has a 10-minute meeting, which they refer to as the 'daily lineup.' During each meeting, they discuss one of their customer service basics such as 'the importance of immaculate attire.' After they've gone through the entire list of basics, they go through it again and again to remind every employee constantly what must be done in order to continually provide impeccable customer service."

Just then a lightbulb seemed to go on inside Phil's head.

"Wait a minute—I think I've finally figured out what you've been trying to tell me all along."

"What's that?" asked Sam.

Phil continued, "On a couple of occasions, as you were explaining some aspect of taming the X-Factor, I would comment with something like, 'Is doing this difficult?' Every time I said that, you would come back with, 'It's not. The only truly difficult thing is remembering to do it!' That's why you have to utilize all these reminder devices—because the most difficult thing associated with any aspect of taming the X-Factor *is* remembering to do it."

"I'm glad you finally made that connection," said Sam, "because it's an extremely important one."

"Sam, I have to admit that I am very impressed," said Phil. "You really have solved the management puzzle. The pieces all fit so tightly together. At this point, I feel ready to try taming the X-Factor on my own."

"I think you would be even more ready if you let me introduce you to a couple of the vice presidents at my company and let them tell you firsthand their experiences in taming the X-Factor."

"That sounds great!" exclaimed Phil.

Once again, Phil pulled out his trusty notepad to record what he had just learned.

Maintenance: A Summary

Renewal is about keeping the excitement necessary to tame the X-Factor from winding down. Keeping this excitement in a constant state of renewal is easy. As a manager, you need to:

1. Maintain your agreements by:

   a. Providing your people with the support necessary to do their jobs well.

   b. Validating your people as winners by celebrating their accomplishments.

2. Maintain your relationships by:

   a. Continuing to do those things that you did to build those relationships with your people in the first place.

  b. Using special occasions as opportunities to bring your people together and have some fun.

3. Maintain your plans by:

  a. Recognizing that the most difficult thing associated with any aspect of taming the X-Factor is remembering to do it.

  b. Creating a system of reminders that prompt you consistently to do those things that are necessary to tame the X-Factor.

Taming the X-Factor with Customers

A t this point, the two men left Sam's office and walked down a hallway to a large wall-less office where they were greeted by a dark-haired, well-dressed woman.

"This is Nancy Kim, our vice president of sales," said Sam. "Thanks to her being able to tame the X-Factor with our customers, we've enjoyed double-digit growth in sales for the past eight consecutive years. I think you'll find her story quite fascinating.

Nancy, I want you to meet Phil Ross, who is visiting with us today."

"Hello," said Nancy as she shook Phil's hand.

"It's a pleasure to meet you," said Phil. "I'm very anxious to hear about your experience in taming the X-Factor with your customers. I must admit, however, that I'm a little puzzled."

"Why is that?" asked Nancy.

"I've never heard of taking a method of managing that was designed to help you manage the people who work for you and applying it to customers," said Phil.

"That's the beauty of taming the X-Factor," said Nancy. "It enables you to manage *anybody* who stands between you and success—whether the person works for you or is another manager, a customer, or a supplier."

"So, how do you apply taming the X-Factor to your customers?" asked Phil.

"With the PRAM Model," replied Nancy with a grin. "The first thing you have to remember is that customers are made up of ordinary people just like us who are motivated out of self-interest. Therefore, everything that Sam has told you about managing the people who work for you also applies to managing customers. The same holds true for managing suppliers and labor unions."

"What I hear you saying," said Phil, "is that once you know how to do it right, managing is managing no matter who you are managing."

"That's it exactly," said Nancy. "You see, I had absolutely no experience in sales before I became vice president of sales, but I did know how to tame the X-Factor, and that's all I needed to be successful."

"This is very exciting," said Phil. "I can't wait to hear your story."

"Let's start at the beginning," said Nancy. "Tell me, do you know what the first step is in developing a plan to tame the X-Factor?"

"To determine your self-interest," answered Phil.

"That's right," said Nancy. "And what do you suppose our self-interest is?"

"To achieve extraordinary results," answered Phil.

"That's correct," said Nancy. "And to achieve extraordinary results in sales, you have to create a certain type of customer. What kind of customer do you think that is?"

"A *satisfied* customer!" exclaimed Phil.

"Wrong!" rejoined Nancy.

"I thought creating satisfied customers was the name of the game when it came to selling," said Phil.

"It is," responded Nancy, "if you want to achieve ordinary results. You see, customers who are merely satisfied are very likely to switch to one of our competitors if they think they can get a better deal. What we're looking to create at this company are *loyal* customers."

"And just what are the benefits of a loyal customer?" asked Phil.

"A loyal customer is excited about doing business with you, is willing to wait in line, and gladly pays premium prices. Furthermore, a loyal customer requires no advertising, doesn't need to be sold over and over, and continually brags about the merits of doing business with you to other potential customers."

"I hear you saying two things," said Phil. "First, when you have loyal customers, you really don't have any competition. Second, when you have loyal customers, they actually function as an extension of your sales force."

"Amen," said Nancy. "More than 80 percent of our business comes to us as the result of repeat business from our loyal customers or from their referring new customers to us."

"Pretty extraordinary, don't you think?" asked Sam with a smile.

"I'll say," said Phil, "but how do you make this happen?"

"By doing the rest of what it takes to tame the X-Factor," responded Nancy. "Once we have clarified our self-interest, the next step is to identify those people in our customer's organization who stand between us and success. We refer to those people as the *key players*. This group would include anyone who could either make or influence the decision of whether the customer uses our company as a supplier. These are the people we must take through all four steps of the PRAM Model, because these are the very people who need to get excited about going the extra mile to help us achieve extraordinary results."

"Who are some of the people that are likely to be included in this group of key players?" asked Phil.

"The list will vary from company to company depending on where the power and influence lie to make buying decisions," replied Nancy. "This list could include one or more people from the purchasing department and possibly someone from the engineering group that is responsible for designing our product into theirs. It could also include certain individuals from the sales, marketing, and quality assurance organizations who are connected with their company's end products that our products go into. This list could also include one or more members of the customer's top management team and may even include certain individuals from their customers' organizations as well."

"Is this list of key players normally a large number of people?" asked Phil.

"Normally, it's not," replied Nancy. "In some cases, it may involve only one or two people. In other situations, it may be as many as five or six. Again, it all depends on how the power and influence are distributed within the customer's organization to make buying decisions."

"Is there any particular process that will enable you to determine accurately who these key players are?" asked Phil.

"As a matter of fact, there is," responded Nancy. She then proceeded to walk over to her flip chart, picked up a marker, and wrote:

```
┌──────────────────────────────────────┐
│                                        │
│                                        │
│               LISTEN                   │
│                                        │
│                                        │
└──────────────────────────────────────┘
```

"You see," said Nancy, "if you can discipline yourself to listen during your initial visits with a customer, it will quickly become apparent who the key players are."

"That sounds easy enough," said Phil.

"You're right," said Nancy. "It does sound like a very easy thing to do, but listening can be very difficult. You see, people by nature are not programmed to listen; they are programmed to talk."

"What I hear you saying," said Phil, "is that listening is something that you and the people in your sales organization have to constantly remind yourselves to do."

"Absolutely," responded Nancy. "When it comes to selling, the more you talk, the less you learn. This is why we ask all of the people in our sales organization to write the word **LISTEN** in bold letters at the top of every page in their notepads. This way, every time they write something down or retrieve something they've already written down, they are reminded that their number one priority is to listen."

Nancy then changed the subject. "Now that we've identified the key players in the customer's organization, what's the next step in developing a plan to tame the X-Factor?"

"To determine the self-interest of each of the key players," answered Phil.

"That's correct," said Nancy. "And what is the self-interest of each of these people?"

"Respect, meaning, and renewal," responded Phil.

"Right, and how do you suppose we go about connecting their self-interest with ours?"

"By executing the remaining three steps of the PRAM Model, which are Relationships, Agreements, and Maintenance," responded Phil.

"And that's *exactly* what we do!" exclaimed Nancy. "Everyone in our sales organization, including our sales managers, our frontline salespeople, and even Sam and me, spends a great deal of time, up front, building relationships with the key players in a customer's organization. You see, it's these relationships that eventually bond our customers to us and lock out our competition."

"Are you saying that you practice Managing By Wandering Around in your customer's plants?" asked Phil.

"Absolutely," replied Nancy. "You have to, if you expect to tame the X-Factor and thus create a loyal customer. The key to building relationships with these key players is more listening. Listening to these people is very important for two reasons. First, listening demonstrates that we take each of these people seriously as individuals—which is what respect is all about. Second, listening to these key players allows us to gather crucial information that we will need in order to successfully execute the Agreements and Maintenance steps of the PRAM Model."

"What sort of information do you gather while you're building these relationships?" asked Phil.

"Anything that will help us become more valuable to the key players in our customer's organization," responded Nancy.

"Like what?" prompted Phil.

"In order to create a loyal customer who will gladly pay premium prices, your value as a supplier has to extend far beyond the products you offer and the prices you charge," said Nancy. "You create this additional value by providing certain things, in addition to your product and price, that enable the key players in the customer's organization to better achieve their goals."

"Like expert advice, special product features,

special services, and special levels of service?" suggested Phil.

"Exactly," replied Nancy. "However, before you can provide these additional things with any degree of effectiveness, you first have to know what the specific goals are for each of the key players and the specific problems and obstacles they must overcome in order to achieve those goals. In order to figure this out, we ask a lot of questions and we listen long and hard. Our goal is to become expert at our customer's business and to get to know each of those key players inside and out including *their personal agendas*."

"Their personal agendas?" repeated Phil, a bit puzzled. "Why would you want to know that?"

"Because it's the most important piece of information there is when it comes to increasing our value to these key players," said Nancy.

"I'm starting to feel lost," admitted Phil.

"Let me see if I can clear this up for you," said Nancy. "A personal agenda represents the preferred ways in which an individual chooses to satisfy his or her need for meaning at work. In other words, it's what a particular individual must do at work in order to validate himself or herself as a winner. As I'm sure Sam has told you, this is an extremely powerful motivator."

"I see now why figuring out a key player's personal agenda is so important," said Phil. "Presenting these people with opportunities to advance their personal agendas and thus satisfy their need for meaning at work is what creates the excitement necessary for you to tame the X-Factor."

"I think he's on a roll," Sam said to Nancy.

Phil continued, "Once you understand what these key players' personal agendas are, all you have to do is tailor what you are offering them in such a way that it comes across as an opportunity for each of them to validate themselves as winners. And when you do this, you've got these people eating right out of your hand."

"You've got it," said Nancy.

"Is figuring out these personal agendas a difficult thing to do?" asked Phil.

"Not at all," said Nancy. "As I mentioned earlier, it takes disciplined listening, but once again the most difficult thing is remembering to look for clues to the key player's personal agenda in what he or she says."

"But isn't each person's personal agenda different?" asked Phil.

"To a certain extent, they are," said Nancy. "But at work, there is one thing that seems to be universal in its appeal, especially among key players, when it comes to an individual's personal agenda."

"What's that?" asked Phil.

Nancy then walked over to her flip chart and began to write. When she finished, the chart read:

```
┌─────────────────────────────────────────┐
│                                           │
│              IMPRESSING                   │
│                 THE                       │
│                BOSS                       │
│                                           │
└─────────────────────────────────────────┘
```

Nancy continued, "If you can tailor what you are offering as something that will enable each of these key players to look like a hero in the eyes of his or her boss, believe me, you are going to get the business."

"This leads right into the Agreements step of the PRAM Model, doesn't it?" asked Phil.

"Yes, it does," answered Nancy. "This is where we connect our self-interest (getting the key players in the customer's organization excited about becoming a loyal customer) with the self-interest of the key players (to satisfy their need for meaning at work by impressing their respective bosses)."

"It seems to me," said Phil, "that this step of the PRAM Model shouldn't be all that difficult given all the information we gathered during the Relationships step."

"You're right," said Nancy. "Because we took the time to gather this information up front, we are now in a position to configure what we call a *Complete*

Customer Solution. A Complete Customer Solution is made up of product features, special services, special levels of service, expert advice, quality assurance, and so forth and is specifically tailored not only to enable the key players to overcome the problems and obstacles that stand between them and the achievement of their goals, but to do so in a way that will enable them to impress their bosses."

"I'll bet the information you gathered during the Relationships step of the PRAM Model also makes presenting this Complete Customer Solution to the key players much more effective, doesn't it?" asked Phil.

"It sure does," responded Nancy. "Since we already know what each of these key players is looking for, all we have to do is present this Complete Customer Solution in such a way that they can easily make the connection between their doing business with us and their being able to impress their bosses. Once they make this connection, believe me, it's over. They're excited, and we've got the business."

"I am truly amazed," said Phil. "You were able to get the business at a premium price and there wasn't even a hint of hard selling involved."

"That's right," said Nancy. "Taming the X-Factor with a customer is not about selling at all. Instead, it's about getting the key players in a customer's organization excited about doing business with you. And remember, the only thing that gets these people excited are opportunities to further their personal agendas. The thing to keep in mind here is that the more excited these key players become, the less of an issue price becomes."

"What I hear you saying," said Phil, "is that when the Complete Customer Solution that you offer the key players includes opportunities for each of them to further their personal agendas, you can then charge more because in their eyes you are well worth it."

"That's it in a nutshell," replied Nancy. "You seem to be developing a really firm grasp on how to tame the X-Factor with customers."

"Does this mean we're ready to move on to the Maintenance step of the PRAM Model?" asked Phil.

"You bet," replied Nancy. "At this point, we've got the key players in the customer's organization excited about becoming a *loyal* customer—a customer who waits in line, gladly pays premium prices, and brags about the merits of doing business with you to other potential customers. If we expect actually to create a loyal customer, it's up to us to keep this excitement from winding down. I'm sure Sam has told you that this is what renewal is all about."

"Yes, he has," replied Phil. "He also told me that keeping this excitement from winding down is simply a matter of maintaining the three things you already have in place." Phil grinned as he walked over toward Nancy's flip chart. Phil then picked up a marker and began to write. When he finished, the chart read:

RENEWAL MEANS YOU

MUST MAINTAIN

- YOUR AGREEMENTS
- YOUR RELATIONSHIPS
- YOUR PLANS

"Well done!" exclaimed Sam. "I can see that you are already anxious for the opportunity to teach others how to tame the X-Factor."

Phil continued, "Let's start at the top of the list with Agreements. You made an agreement with the key players in the customer's organization, either implicitly or explicitly, to provide them with an opportunity to advance their personal agendas and thus satisfy their need for meaning at work in exchange for their getting excited about becoming a loyal customer. One extremely important aspect of keeping this excitement alive is to make sure that you hold up your end of this agreement."

"Right," said Nancy. "This is especially true when you consider that some or all of these key players may have put their necks on the line in order to give us the business at a premium price. We've got to make these people look like heroes to their bosses for having done so, and that's exactly what we do."

"Is this a difficult thing to pull off?" asked Phil.

"Not at all," answered Nancy. "We know exactly what they expect from us in terms of performance because we helped to create those expectations. All we have to do, then, is to perform in such a way that we exceed their expectations and everybody wins: The key players further their personal agendas by impressing their bosses, and we're well on our way to having created a loyal customer."

"What I hear you saying," said Phil, "is that you maintain your agreements with the key players in the customer's organization by *earning* those premium prices you're charging."

"Amen," said Nancy. "That makes their paying premium prices a win-win situation, doesn't it?"

"It sure does," agreed Phil. "I'm starting to see why you've enjoyed double-digit growth in sales for the past eight consecutive years. By making it a practice of exceeding expectations and causing key players to look like heroes to their bosses, you give your customers every reason to continue to do business with you, and you also give them a lot to say when they talk to other potential customers about you."

"That's what it's all about," said Nancy with a smile. "Now that you understand maintaining agreements, it's time to talk about maintaining our relationships with these key players in our customer's organization. What do you suppose that is all about?"

Phil thought for a minute and then responded, "To continue to practice Managing By Wandering Around with those key players in the customer's organization to make sure that the trust you worked so hard to put in place doesn't start to fade away."

"That's it exactly," said Nancy. "We continue to visit with these key players regularly and often. Again, the emphasis in these visits is on listening for the same two very important things that we listened to while we were building these relationships."

"Let me guess," interrupted Phil. "First, listening reinforces the notion that you care, that you do take each of these key players seriously as individuals—which is what respect is all about. Second, listening allows us to gather information that will be crucial for successfully executing the Agreements and Maintenance steps of the PRAM Model in the future."

"Right you are," said Nancy. "You see, over time things in a customer's organization can change considerably: The nature of the customer's business can change, the bosses of the key players can change, and the key players themselves can change. This could mean that what it will take for the key players to impress their bosses in the future may be totally different than what it takes today. Listening to these people on a regular and frequent basis enables us to detect these changes early so that we can make the necessary adjustments in our Complete Customer Solution, and thus keep the excitement level among the key players from winding down."

"What I hear you telling me," said Phil, "is that you can't become complacent if you expect to maintain the loyalty of your customers over the long term."

"Absolutely!" exclaimed Nancy. "If there is one thing that history in our business has taught us over and over, it is that the death knell for a loyal customer begins when you stop listening to the key players in that customer's organization."

"What still amazes me," remarked Phil, "is that everything you've mentioned so far about taming the X-Factor with a customer is really quite simple to do, and yet the payoff for doing these simple things is really phenomenal."

"That's right," said Nancy. "The only truly difficult aspect of taming the X-Factor with a customer—" She looked at Phil and paused as she waited for him to finish the sentence.

Phil smiled and said, "Remembering to do these simple things."

"Exactly," said Nancy. "That's why in our sales

organization, we pay a great deal of attention to the final aspect of renewal, which is maintaining our plans. You see, visiting the key players in a customer's organization, listening to them long and hard, and then making adjustments in a Complete Customer Solution that seems to be working very well at the moment are not automatic behaviors. In other words, you can't assume that just because you understand all the things that are necessary to tame the X-Factor with a customer you are automatically going to engage in the correct behavior whenever the situation calls for it. This is especially true when things are going well, because then there is a strong natural tendency to become complacent—which is the precursor to not listening to the key players in the customer's organization. The only way you can make sure that you consistently engage in these behaviors is to continually remind yourself to do so."

"How do you go about making sure that happens?" asked Phil.

"I expect everyone in our sales organization, including our sales managers and our frontline salespeople as well as myself, to ask themselves a question a minimum of three times during the day," replied Nancy. "Do you have any idea what that question might be?"

Phil thought for a few seconds and then smiled. "Well," he said, "since taming the X-Factor with the key players in a customer's organization is no different from taming the X-Factor with the people who work for you, there is only one thing it can be." Phil then walked over to Nancy's flip chart, flipped over the top page, and began to write. When he finished, the chart read:

```
AM I BEHAVING
LIKE A GREAT
MANAGER?
```

"That's it!" exclaimed Nancy. "We have found in our sales organization that the best times to answer this question are when you first come to work, right after lunch, and right before you call it a day. If you can discipline yourself to do this, you'll find that it really does keep you on course. We also utilize the same visual reminders that I'm sure Sam has shared with you—like having the PRAM Model on our name badges and business cards, using the PRAM Model as a screen saver on our computer monitors, and wearing X-shaped pins on our lapels. I fully agree with Sam that you can't have too many reminders around that prompt you to do the right things."

"Do you hold X-Meetings in your sales organization as well?" asked Phil.

"Yes, we do," responded Nancy. "The ideal situation would be for me to meet daily with our sales managers and for them to meet daily with the frontline salespeople who work for them. However, since everyone in our sales organization is spread out all across the country, this is impossible. But I do meet face-to-face with each of our sales managers as often as I can, and they do the same thing with the frontline salespeople who work for them. Again, the emphasis during these meetings is to make sure that we are all consistently doing those things that are necessary to tame the X-Factor with the key players in our customer's organizations, which in turn leads to the creation of more and more loyal customers for our company."

"Sam said I would find your story fascinating, and he was right," said Phil. "Thank you so much for taking the time to share it with me."

"It was pleasure," said Nancy as she shook hands with Phil.

"Keep up the good work, Nancy," said Sam as he shook her hand. "And thanks for taking the time."

CHAPTER

10

Taming the X-Factor with a Labor Union

———

A s the two men left Nancy's office, Phil asked, "Where do we go from here?"

"I'm quite convinced that you are now ready to go out and tame the X-Factor on your own, but there is one more person I want you to talk with before you leave," said Sam.

Sam then directed Phil toward another open office where they were greeted by a gentleman whom Sam introduced as Fritz Gallow.

"Fritz is our vice president of labor relations. Fritz and I worked together as a team to tame the X-Factor with our labor union. Thanks to Fritz's hard work in leading this effort, we have a 15-year labor agreement in place and we've enjoyed double-digit productivity gains for the past eight years running. Fritz, I want you to meet Phil Ross, who is visiting us today. Nancy and I have been telling him about the X-Factor."

"Glad to meet you," said Fritz as he shook Phil's hand.

"The same here," said Phil. "I am extremely anxious to hear your story because at my company we do not do a good job of managing our labor union."

"Since you've already heard the full-blown version of how to tame the X-Factor, I'll just hit the high spots from my perspective," said Fritz.

"That sounds fine to me," said Phil.

Fritz continued, "The first thing you have to remember when you try to tame the X-Factor with a labor union is that unions are made up of ordinary people like the three of us who are motivated out of self-interest. Therefore, everything that Sam and Nancy told you about taming the X-Factor also applies to managing labor unions. I had absolutely no experience in dealing with unions before I became vice president of labor relations, but I did know how to tame the X-Factor—and that's all I needed to make this effort successful."

"It's amazing how taming the X-Factor has such universal applicability," said Phil.

"Let's start at the beginning," said Fritz. "When Sam took over as president of this company 10 years ago, the place was in a shambles and in serious danger of closing its doors for good. Productivity gains were nonexistent, the union was on strike with scores of grievances pending, and morale around here was in the pits. We began with the Plans step of the PRAM Model, and the first step in planning was to determine our self-interest—that is the extraordinary results that we wanted to achieve. Sam and I quickly concluded that we wanted to eliminate the present situation by creating a loyal hourly-wage workforce that was committed to achieving significant productivity gains."

"That almost sounds like *Mission Impossible*," commented Phil.

"It sure seemed like it at the time," replied Fritz, "but as usual the PRAM Model was up to the challenge. Our next step in planning was to determine those people in the union's organization who stood between us and success or failure. Like Nancy, we refer to these people as *key players*. This group of people would include anyone who could either make or influence the union's decision to work with us or against us. These are the people we needed to take through all four steps of the PRAM Model, because these were the people we needed to get excited about helping us achieve the extraordinary results we were looking for."

"Did you know, up front, who these key players were?"

"Not really," answered Fritz. "We knew that some of the elected officials were likely to be key players, but we weren't sure who. We also knew there were key players among the membership of the union who were not elected officials."

"How did you go about figuring this out?" asked Phil.

"Lots of listening," responded Fritz. "We knew that listening would pay off for us in three very important ways. First, we knew that if we listened to what the membership of the union had to say, it would quickly become apparent who the key players were. Second, we knew that listening to what these very unhappy people had to say and then doing something about it would go a long way toward restoring the trust that was missing. Third, we knew listening would allow us to gather important information that we could use to complete the Plans step of the PRAM Model and also to effectively execute the Agreements and Maintenance steps."

"What I hear you saying," said Phil, "is that when you ran out of information that was necessary to complete the Plans step of the PRAM Model, you jumped right into the Relationships step to gather this information."

"Very perceptive," replied Fritz. "That's exactly what we did."

"How did you go about getting started?" asked Phil.

"We started out by having lots of open meetings for union members. At these meetings, we asked the attendees for their input and opinions on how things ought to be done at this company, and we were very emphatic that we didn't want them to hold back. As it turned out, they had lots of opinions and lots of anger to vent besides, but we listened, we took notes, and we took action."

"What happened?" asked Phil.

"During that first year or so we, as the expression goes, 'picked a lot of low-hanging fruit.' For example, the membership of the union unanimously felt that the company rest rooms were substandard. We took one look and agreed. We asked the union to put together a committee to make recommendations as to how they thought the rest rooms should be brought up to standard. We then took those recommendations and renovated the rest rooms just the way they wanted them. We took the same approach when the union's membership said the work areas were dirty and dingy, and renovated those areas to their satisfaction. They told us that not having a paved parking lot caused a lot of people to get their cars stuck in the mud when it rained, so we paved the parking lot—and so forth and so on. All the while this was going on, we continued to meet."

Fritz added, "It didn't take too long before it was obvious who the key players in the union were, because they took over directing all the discussions at these meetings. The next thing we knew, the key players suggested that we start meeting solely with them instead of having the open meetings with the entire membership. This was very good from our perspective because now we were meeting exclusively with the people who stood between us and success or failure."

"Why did the key players want to do that?" asked Phil.

"To enhance their status as leaders within the union organization," replied Fritz. "When we met only with the key players, every time they brought us a request from their membership that we subsequently acted upon they could claim credit to their membership for having brought about that change."

"So looking good to their membership while performing their roles as leaders is a personal agenda item for these key players?" asked Phil.

"Absolutely," responded Fritz. "In fact, it's the most important personal agenda item to these key players because they really want to hang onto their roles as leaders within the union organization."

"Did the trust that you and Sam were hoping for between management and the key players in the union ever materialize?" asked Phil.

"Yes, it did," responded Fritz, "but it took a while. Every time a suggestion was brought to us from the union membership by the key players and we acted on it in such a way that the key players looked like heroes to their membership, we nudged the trust level we were looking for a little closer to reality. We knew we had come a long way toward gaining their trust when one day, during a meeting, a key player allowed a personal agenda item to surface."

"What was that?" asked Phil.

"Sam and I had spent numerous meetings trying to impress upon these key players that we needed significant productivity gains from the union membership if we expected to stay in business over the long term. Up until then, our pleading seemed to have no impact on these key players. At this point, one of the key union players said, 'Do you know what would really make a difference here? If we, the union, could have a piece of the action. In other words, if we work hard to achieve those productivity gains that you are looking for in order to make the company more profitable, some of those additional profits that we helped create ought to come back to us in the form of a bonus.' This key player paused for a moment and continued, 'In fact, if you—management—can come up with a bonus clause we can live with, I guarantee we will find the productivity gains you are looking for, because we know right where they are.'"

"Amazing," said Phil. "That person just told you what it would take to make all the key players look like superheroes to their union's membership—a bonus clause that would put serious money in everyone's pockets in exchange for the productivity gains you were looking for."

"That's right," said Fritz. "Sam and I were ecstatic because we knew that the remaining aspects of taming the X-Factor with our labor union were going to be quite easy."

"Did everything work out the way that you hoped?" asked Phil.

"It sure did," replied Fritz. "We moved immediately to the Agreements step of the PRAM Model where we connected our two sets of self-interests— the bonus clause the key players from the union were looking for and the productivity gains we were looking for. The key players then presented this idea to their membership, where it was very well received, thus making them look like heroes. We then succeeded in creating the loyal hourly-wage workforce we were looking for that was committed to achieving significant productivity gains by doing an excellent job with the Maintenance step of the PRAM Model."

"Let me guess," interrupted Phil. "You held up your end of the agreement, which meant that when the agreed-upon productivity gains were achieved, the union membership got the bonus checks they were expecting."

"Absolutely," said Fritz. "We also celebrated those achievements in such a way that the entire union membership felt like heroes, and we continue to do the same today. Sam and I also maintain our relationships with these key people by continuing to have regular meetings with them and by practicing Managing By Wandering Around with them. Our emphasis during both these activities is on listening. As I'm sure both Sam and Nancy have told you, listening is critical for two reasons. First, it sends these people a very clear message that you take each of them seriously as individuals. Second, listening enables you to gather information that will be crucial to taming the X-Factor in the future."

Fritz continued, "Sam and I maintain our plans by employing all kinds of reminders—from X-Meetings to asking ourselves three times a day, 'Am I behaving like a great manager?'—in order to make sure we don't overlook the most difficult aspect of taming the X-Factor—which is remembering to do it."

"Thank you so much for sharing your experience with me. I have learned a lot," said Phil.

"It was a pleasure," said Fritz as he shook Phil's hand.

"Thanks for taking the time, Fritz," said Sam as he shook Fritz's hand.

"See you at the X-Meeting in the morning," said Fritz as he watched the two men leave his office.

The End of a Great Morning

As the two men walked back toward Sam's office, Phil was very excited. "What a great morning! I not only learned the solution to the management puzzle, which is taming the X-Factor, but I also learned that you can use this solution to manage everything from the people who work for you, to customers, to labor unions."

"We also use it to manage our suppliers," said Sam. "Taming the X-Factor with our suppliers has transformed our supply management organization from one that used to beat suppliers up over price to one that generates a significant amount of sales for our company. I would have loved to have introduced you to Katherine Nielsen, our vice president of supply management, so that you could have heard her story, but she's out on a trip visiting some of our suppliers in Asia. So we'll have to catch her at another time."

"I am truly impressed at how simple taming the X-Factor is and how tightly all the pieces fit together," said Phil. "But do you know what the most valuable lesson that I learned today is?"

"What's that?"

"How the toughest part of taming the X-Factor is not the effort required," answered Phil. "It's *remembering to do* the simple things that enable you to tame it."

Phil then reached out to shake Sam's hand. "I can't thank you enough for all you've done for me today."

"Believe me, it was a pleasure," said Sam. "You are on your way to becoming a great manager. Please stay in touch."

He Became a Great Manager: A Summary

Phil Ross went on to become a truly great manager because he never forgot all the valuable management lessons that Sam had taught him:

1. The X-Factor is about getting ordinary people X-cited about going the X-tra mile to help you, the manager, achieve X-traordinary results.

2. The basic elements of the X-Factor are *people* and *motivation*.

3. People are universally motivated by *self-interest*.

4. The PRAM Model is the prescription for taming the X-Factor.

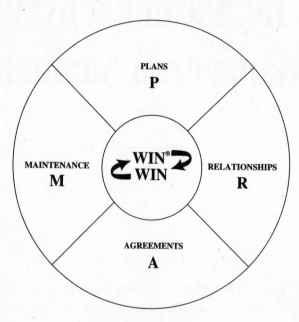

The PRAM Model
R$_x$ for Taming the X-Factor

5. The PRAM Model is circular to remind us that taming the X-Factor is a continuous, ongoing process.

6. "WIN-WIN" is at the core of the PRAM Model because all aspects of taming the X-Factor must be win-win.

7. Taming the X-Factor involves properly executing the four steps of the PRAM Model.

Step One: Plans

Developing a Plan to tame the X-Factor is simple. As a manager, you need to:

1. Determine your self-interest, which is achieving extraordinary results.

2. Identify those people who stand between you and success.

3. Determine their self-interest.

   a. Respect.

   b. Meaning.

   c. Renewal.

4. Execute the remaining three steps of the PRAM Model to connect the two sets of self-interest.

Step Two: Relationships

Before people can get excited about helping their manager achieve extraordinary results, they must first feel that their manager respects them as individuals. Showing respect is easy. As a manager, you need to build Relationships with your people that lead to trust. You do this by:

1. Regularly and frequently circulating among your people.

2. Asking for their thoughts and opinions.

3. Listening to what they have to say.

4. Taking whatever constructive action is required.

Step Three: Agreements

Meaning is what creates the excitement necessary to tame the X-Factor. Creating opportunities for people to satisfy their need for meaning at work is easy. As a manager, you need to reach an Agreement with your people concerning:

1. What things do we want to become the *best* at?

2. How do we define *best*?

3. How do we go about becoming the *best* at the things we've chosen?

Step Four: Maintenance

Renewal is about keeping the excitement necessary to tame the X-Factor from winding down. Keeping this excitement in a constant state of renewal is easy. As a manager, you need to:

1. Maintain your agreements by:

   a. Providing your people with the support necessary to do their jobs well.

   b. Validating your people as winners by celebrating their accomplishments.

2. Maintain your relationships by:

   a. Continuing to do those things that you did to build those relationships with your people in the first place.

   b. Using special occasions as opportunities to bring your people together and have some fun.

3. Maintain your plans by:

   a. Recognizing that the most difficult thing associated with any aspect of taming the X-Factor is remembering to do it.

   b. Creating a system of reminders that prompt you consistently to do those things that are necessary to tame the X-Factor.

Yes, Phil Ross had accomplished his goal. He had found the solution to the management puzzle.

Appendixes

Putting the X-Factor to Work

A t this point you are probably saying to yourself, "Okay, that was nice little story, logically presented, and the X-Factor seems to make perfect sense—but does it hold up in the real world?"

To answer this question, I have included a number of real world examples of companies and individuals that have successfully tamed the X-Factor. These examples validate the effectiveness as well as the versatility of the X-Factor and illustrate how anyone can use it to achieve his or her own set of extraordinary results. As you read through these examples, keep in mind that the essence of taming the X-Factor is engaging the self-interest of the people who stand between you and success or failure. This involves identifying their self-interest and then connecting it with yours, which is to achieve extraordinary results.

The Secret Behind America's Best-Run Airline

As was mentioned in the Introduction, Southwest Airlines is one of the most respected and admired American businesses. The question is, how does the airline do it? The answer is simple. Southwest Airlines, more than any other major company, has succeeded in taming the X-Factor with its employees. The management at Southwest thoroughly understands the three components of work-related self-interest—respect, meaning, and renewal—and does something about it.

For example, respect for the individual is a way of life at Southwest. Management walks the talk that employees come first, not customers. Employees are viewed as family members. According to chief executive officer (CEO) Herb Kelleher, "A family atmosphere simply means that you are sincerely interested in everyone who's a part of your family." The company's firm no-layoff policy also sends a strong message that Southwest cares about its employees.

Southwest employees work very hard and no one complains, because their work has meaning. They view their work as a mission, and that mission is freedom—to open up the skies so that average people can afford to fly. These employees are excited about working for Southwest because they know that what they do makes a difference in other people's lives.

The management of Southwest Airlines also takes renewal very seriously. Managers realize that employees cannot sustain high levels of effort and excitement without having their batteries recharged. Southwest makes extensive use of celebrations to keep its workforce energized. Managers and workers celebrate everything—group and individual achievements, birthdays, anniversaries, and promotions—and they have a passion for doing it right. Southwest also has a strong corporate culture that serves as a constant reminder to all who work there to keep doing those necessary things that produce the extraordinary results.

Getting Tough Customers to Listen

Several years ago, I did some consulting work for the sales organization of a large pharmaceutical company. These people were very concerned with the fact that one of their new products wasn't selling very well. The product was a timed-release patch for managing pain that was used by chemotherapy patients. This product was an alternative to morphine, and the company's clinical studies showed that it was a superior product because it was far less addictive and had fewer side effects. The problem was that doctors weren't prescribing it, and these people wanted me to help them figure out why.

In an attempt to find the answer, I put this problem through the planning process that is necessary to tame the X-Factor. The first question I asked was, "Who are the people who stand between you and success or failure?"

Their answer was, "Oncologists—doctors who specialize in the treatment of cancer."

I then asked, "What do you want from these people?"

"To prescribe our product," they answered.

"What do these oncologists want from you?" I asked. "What is their self-interest?"

"A pain management system that's less addictive and has fewer side effects than morphine," they replied.

My next comment was, "How do you try to sell this product to the oncologists?"

"We pull out the results of our clinical trials and show them how our product is a superior pain management system compared to morphine," they answered.

"Do these oncologists appear interested in what you have to say about your product?" I asked.

The answer was, "Not at all! It's like they're not even listening to what we're saying."

At this point I said, "The very fact that these oncologists aren't listening to what you have to say about your product strongly indicates that the way in which you are presenting your product is not connecting with the oncologists' self-interest."

I then suggested that maybe they had misassessed these oncologists' self-interest and that maybe the oncologists weren't as interested in pain management as they thought. In order to get a better idea of what the oncologists' self-interest really was, I asked, "Is pain management the primary concern of an oncologist?"

These people thought for a moment and then answered, "Not really. The primary concern of an oncologist is *curing the patient.*"

"There's your problem" I suggested. "You have a group of physicians (oncologists) who are extremely busy and primarily concerned with one thing (curing their patients), and you want them to take valuable time out of their day to listen to what you have to say about pain management? It's not so surprising they're not listening."

I then went on to say, "If you want these doctors

to listen to what you have to say about your product, you have to present it in such a way that it connects with *their* self-interest. So instead of presenting this product as a superior pain management system compared to morphine, I suggest you present it as either part of the cure itself or as an enhancement to the cure."

I pointed out that with this approach they could take the busiest, most important oncologist who has absolutely no time for pharmaceutical sales representatives and stop this person in his or her tracks with a presentation like, "Doctor, I know you're busy, but I've got something here that will significantly extend the lives of your patients."

At this point the sales rep will have succeeded in capturing the oncologist's undivided attention because he or she is addressing something that is very important to the oncologist. More than likely, the oncologist will take the necessary time to listen to everything the sales rep has to say about this product. This affords the sales rep the opportunity to tell the oncologist that since this product is less addictive than morphine with fewer side effects, patients can stay on the treatment longer and more of them will be able to see the treatment through to completion; this means a patient can get back to a happier and more productive life more quickly. Once the oncologist understands these benefits, the sales rep can point out that all the oncologist has to do to accrue these benefits is to prescribe this product. When the sales force used this approach, sales of this product took off like a rocket.

The lesson here is that once you correctly figure out the true self-interest of the people who stand between you and success or failure, it's easier to get them to say yes.

Hanging on to Wealthy Clients

A senior vice president of a bank for whom I was doing some consulting came to me one day crying the blues. His concern was that some of the competing banks had decided to aggressively go after some of the large depositors who did business with his branch banks located in several wealthy retirement communities. The way in which these competing banks were trying to lure these wealthy customers away was by offering them significantly higher interest rates if they would switch banks. The senior vice president went on the say he felt that the only way he could hang on to these very important customers was to match or beat the higher rates being offered by his competition. He was reluctant to do this, however, because it would be expensive and it would probably trigger a price war that would eventually result in none of the competitors making any money.

I suggested that if he didn't want to lose these valuable customers, he'd have to give them a reason to stay. I went on to tell him that matching the competition on interest was one way to do this, but it was probably not getting at the real reason these people were leaving. I pointed out that a very important self-interest of elderly wealthy people was to be treated in special ways that singled them out as being wealthy. I further suggested that, given their ages, probably all of these people had more than enough money to last them for the rest of their lives, so a few dollars more was not likely to be a long-term motivator of their behavior.

In order to engage these elderly wealthy depositors' self-interest, I suggested he give them some very special attention and basically ignore the interest rate increases being offered by the competition. We came up with a program to organize gala events for these people on a quarterly basis—elegant afternoon tea parties, for example. These parties were announced to the targeted customers using engraved invitations. The tea and hors d'oeuvres were served with fine china and silver. In addition, the president of the bank and several of the officers were on hand at each of these events to mingle with the guests.

These events have been a smashing success. Instead of losing any of these elderly wealthy customers, the bank actually began to attract new customers as the result of referrals from people who had attended some of the parties. This was truly win-win in action: The customers got what they wanted—special treatment that appealed to their self-interest—and the senior vice president got what he wanted, in that he was able to hang on to these customers without having to match the interest rates being offered by the competition. Furthermore, the cost of the parties was insignificant compared to the cost of meeting the competition's higher interest rates.

Connecting Self-Interest by Actions When You Can't with Words

A territory sales rep for Upjohn communicated with her actions when she was denied the opportunity to communicate with words. She was making a joint sales call with her boss, the district manager. The doctor they were calling on worked at a medical clinic that was located on the twelfth floor of a high-rise office building in downtown Los Angeles. It's important to remember here that most doctors don't like to meet with pharmaceutical sales reps for several reasons: There are lots of them; they are young and aggressive; they think they know everything, so they insult the doctor's intelligence; and they often promise things on which they don't follow through.

When they arrived at this clinic, the doctor they wanted to see made it very clear through his receptionist that he had no intention of seeing them. As they stood there trying to figure out what to do next, the very doctor they wanted to see came out of the examining area and said, "I have a woman patient in one of my examining rooms who would like a videotape on Rogaine. Do you have a videotape with you that I could give her right now?"

Since they didn't have one in their immediate possession, the doctor went back into the examining room without even listening to what they had to say. The sales rep did have a videotape on Rogaine in the trunk of her car. But that was down 12 floors, across the street, down the street two blocks, and down four floors in a parking garage.

Nevertheless, this sales rep immediately set off to retrieve that tape. When she returned, her boss was standing outside the entrance to the building. The woman who wanted the tape had already left, but the sales rep's boss knew what she was wearing and which direction she was walking. They caught up with this woman and gave her the videotape, a gesture for which she was very grateful. They then went back to the medical clinic, where the sales rep wrote a detailed memo concerning what she had done. She then stapled her business card to the memo and left it with the receptionist.

Two days later, the sales rep's phone rang. Guess who it was? It was the very doctor who just two days earlier would not agree to meet with her. And guess what he wanted her to do? He wanted her to make an appointment to come in and meet with him. Why? Because with that single gesture she had convinced this doctor that she was the type of sales rep that had his best interest at heart. That's the kind of sales rep every doctor wants to work with.

The lesson here is that this sales rep went from no access to total access based on a single gesture that connected her self-interest (seeing the doctor) with his self-interest (having a sales rep that he could rely on).

Learning How to Charge Premium Prices

A number of years ago, shortly after I completed my Ph.D., I decided I wanted to get into the consulting and training business. I had picked up a few small jobs, but nothing of any great size. Finally, my chance came to land what I considered a biggie. The job involved 40 days of training per year for an indefinite number of years. I was excited and started putting a selling strategy together to make sure I landed this job. I *assumed*, as there were lots of good consultant/trainers running around, that I was in a very competitive situation and therefore the only thing that mattered to the customer was the price. Thus I decided I would lower my already low asking price by 25 percent in order to make sure I would have a fighting chance to land this job. The first order of business was to meet with the corporate staff who had the authority to hire me.

I arrived at the corporate headquarters on a Monday morning at 8:15 to be interviewed and, I hoped, to negotiate the price and terms of an agreement. I was met in the lobby by one of the members of the corporate staff who informed me that the meeting would start a half hour later than originally scheduled. The reason for this was that the corporate staff was supposed to have met the previous Friday to plan jointly the meeting with me. However, the president called them into another meeting, which lasted past 5:30 P.M., and the planning meeting concerning me never took place. This staff member apologized for inconveniencing me and took me to his office where he told me to make myself at home until the meeting started

As it turned out, this staff person had a secretary who was very friendly and personable. After we had talked for a while, I felt comfortable asking her some questions about the training program. When I asked if her company had ever conducted such a training program in the past, she told me they had during the previous year, but it had ended in disaster. She went on to say that the instructors had done such a poor job that the program participants had gotten up and walked out before noon on the first day of the program. Moreover, she informed me that the corporate staff was really under the gun to find a quality instructor this time, because the president himself was going to sit in on the program to make sure it was done right. She also volunteered that because one of the staff members had attended one of my seminars during the previous year, I was the only person they were considering for the job!

As you can see, my initial assumptions could not have been more wrong. This staff's main concern (self-interest) was not low price; it was whether I would make them look good enough in front of the president to get them out of the doghouse. If I could convince them that I would do just that, the job would be mine and price would not even be an issue (as long as it was within reason). I immediately raised my asking price by 50 percent and quickly developed a strategy to convince the corporate staff that I would make them look good in front of the president. I got the job, and the price I asked was not even questioned. The president loved the program, the corporate staff got out of the doghouse, and I went on to do business with this company for 14 straight years, picking up numerous referrals along the way.

Once you figure out the self-interests of the people who stand between you and success or failure, achieving the outcome you want is quite easy.

How the IBM Legend Was Built

During the 1970s and 1980s, IBM dominated the computer industry. The reason for this was that IBM knew exactly what it wanted from its customers. IBM wanted its customers to buy computers, to keep buying them, and to refer new customers to IBM. IBM also knew what its customers wanted from IBM. IBM's customers didn't normally want the world's best computer. In fact, most of these customers would have been hard-pressed to explain what the world's best computer was. What these customers did want was a computer that would take care of their needs in a very satisfactory manner. More importantly, however, IBM knew that the self-interest of their customers was that they didn't want to look bad for having made the decision to purchase IBM equipment. Rather, they wanted to look like heroes. When they made the decision to purchase IBM equipment, what they were actually buying was the security of knowing that if anything were to break down or go wrong, IBM would take care of the situation in very short order. In fact, IBM built its service reputation back then by doing things like flying in parts on a Learjet to make sure broken-down computer equipment was up and running by the next day. This level of service gave rise to the saying, "Nobody ever got fired by buying an IBM."

Knowing this, IBM proceeded to connect its customers' self-interest (high need for security) with its self-interest (market domination) by providing its customers with a computer that was adequate for the customer's needs along with a *phenomenal* level of service. In return, IBM's customers provided IBM with a high level of repeat and referral business, and were very eager to volunteer positive testimonials and accolades about the benefits of doing business with IBM. What's more, these customers paid premium prices for the privilege of doing business with IBM and enabled IBM to dominate the market.

A Neighborhood Restaurant Extraordinaire

A Mexican restaurant in my neighborhood called Mi Amigo's is a master at connecting its self-interest with the self-interest of its customers. The management realizes that children often have a strong influence on where the family is going to dine— especially during the week. The management also realizes that what really influences the children's decision (their self-interest) is not so much the food, although the food has to be acceptable to them, but any special treatment that is directed specifically at them. Thus, when the meal is ended, the management takes some extra steps to make sure that the children remember their dining experience at Mi Amigo's in a very positive way. First, when the waitress brings the check, she also brings a delicious chocolate mint candy for everyone at the table. This is the highlight of the children's evening, and they are all smiles. But there's more to come. On the way out, there is the hostess holding a large basket filled with lollipops, and each child is allowed to reach in and choose the one he or she wants.

As inexpensive and mundane as these little gestures may seem to you, they are incredibly effective for connecting the self-interest of the children (special treatment) with the self-interest of the restaurant (repeat and referral business). Whenever Mom and Dad are too tired to cook dinner and the decision is made to eat out, the first thing out of the children's mouths is, "Let's go to Mi Amigo's!" I can assure you that these management gestures work on other families besides ours. Whenever you arrive at Mi Amigo's after 6:00 P.M., you can bet there will be a line, but it's a line most kids don't mind waiting in.

The High Cost of a Big Ego

During a recent seminar, I was confronted with a situation that involved an account manager who was trying to get a certain doctor to speak at a conference he was sponsoring. The problem was that this particular doctor charged $5,000 for a speech and the account manager had only $2,500 in the budget. Compounding the situation was that this doctor's ego (a form of self-interest) was tied to his fee. The account manager's question to me was, "How do I get this doctor to speak for $2,500?"

I must admit, I didn't have a clue. Fortunately, one of the other account managers in the room had the answer. "I got that same doctor to speak for free two years ago and his fee was $5,000 then, too."

Of course, everyone in the room wanted to know how he did it. The account manager went on to say that the first thing he did was stroke this doctor's ego by saying, "Obviously, you are worth your fee or you couldn't charge it. So I don't blame you for turning me down." He further appealed to this doctor's ego by informing him that a very famous surgeon whom this doctor had studied under and deeply admired as a mentor was going to be attending this conference. He then informed this doctor that he had jumped the gun a bit by telling the surgeon that this doctor was going to be one of the featured speakers at the conference, and the surgeon was really looking forward to hearing this doctor's talk. The account manager said to the doctor, "This surgeon is going to be very disappointed when I tell him that you are not going to be on the program."

When the doctor heard this, he volunteered to speak at the conference for free. Why? Because the account manager had offered him something that doctor's ego was tied to even more strongly than his $5,000 speaking fee—a chance to show off in front of his mentor!

The lesson here is that many people will trade off money for ego gratification and see it very much as a win-win situation.

Figuring Out Others' Self-Interest

How does one go about the business of identifying another person's self-interest? The key discipline is *listening*. If you listen long enough, another human being will tell you exactly what his or her self-interest is. Effective listening involves the following sequence of behaviors:

- Ask questions.

- Listen to the customer's response.

- Summarize in your mind what the customer said.

- Feed this summary back to the other person.

- Ask follow-up questions, and repeat the process.

Several years ago, I was involved in a consulting project with a pharmaceutical company that was coming out with a new product. The target customers for this new product were radiology administrators of hospitals. Before this product was launched, the company conducted 21 interviews with radiology administrators in three major cities across the United States. Each interview lasted 45 minutes and was conducted by a professional interviewer in a room where one of the walls consisted of one-way glass. I, along with a market research team, sat on the other side of the one-way glass from the interviewer and the radiology administrator. We could see them, but they couldn't see us.

The way the interviewer conducted each interview was that he asked the radiology administrator questions, listened attentively to the answers, and every so often would feed back a summary of what had been said. Then he would ask follow-up questions and do the same thing again.

For example, the interviewer might ask, "How do you go about the business of picking a certain pharmaceutical product over its competitors?" The interviewer would then listen to what the radiology administrator had to say, and when he thought it was appropriate he would feed back a summary of what had been said (e.g., "What I hear you saying is that pharmacoeconomic value is a more important criterion for deciding what product to purchase than the actual price"). The interviewer would then ask a couple of follow-up questions (e.g., "Is this true? Are there any other important criteria for choosing which product to buy?") and then repeat the process.

What was the payoff for all this listening? In all 21 interviews, each radiology administrator told the professional interviewer (a total stranger) *exactly* what it would take (his self-interest) to get his business.

The preceding example clearly illustrates that if you can discipline yourself to listen and let the other person do most of the talking, it won't take you too long to figure out his or her self-interest.

My experience has shown me time and again that people are dying to tell you what's really important to them. The problem is that nobody is listening.

The Value of a Reminder System

I'm going to close these examples off with a final reminder that none of the behaviors associated with taming the X-Factor are reflex managerial behaviors. In other words, you cannot assume that just because you understand all the things that are necessary to tame the X-Factor you are automatically going to engage in the correct behavior whenever the situation calls for it. The only way you can make sure that you consistently engage in these behaviors is to develop a system that reminds you to do so, whether it be holding daily meetings like Ritz-Carlton Hotel Company, hanging PRAM posters on your office wall, or asking yourself three times a day, "Am I behaving like a great manager?" Without such a system, you simply won't succeed at taming the X-Factor.

Shannon Roney, vice president of a company called EMDS, found X-Meetings to be a useful way for keeping her sales staff on track. As Shannon puts it, "For several years, sales at EMDS were steady but flat. The last two years showed a dramatic decline in sales due to fierce competitive pressures. We were losing our customers and not bringing new ones in. We tried numerous approaches to increase our sales, but nothing worked. It was then that I learned about X-Meetings. I immediately began holding brief sales meetings *three times a day* to discuss our strategy and relationship management. After two years of holding these meetings, our sales have gone up 203 percent. Today, we continue to hold the meetings, and our sales curve continues to point upward. It's truly amazing how well these X-Meetings work."

Using the PRAM Model as a Diagnostic Tool

O ne of the important advantages of the PRAM Model is that it is incredibly useful as a diagnostic and problem-solving tool. I haven't found a human interaction problem yet where I couldn't pinpoint the cause of the problem within one of the four steps of the PRAM Model. A problem can be a planning problem, a relationship problem, an agreement problem, or a maintenance problem, and once you locate its true cause, you are then in a position to prescribe an appropriate course of action to resolve the problem. Several brief examples of how to use the PRAM Model as a diagnostic tool follow.

A Teenager with a Behavior Problem at School

I have a friend who is a telemarketer and schedules speaking engagements for me. One day she called to ask me tentatively to hold a date for a program in Tucson. After we had finished our business, I decided it was time to do a little relationship maintenance with her. So I asked her how it was going. She told me things had been going fine until that afternoon when the school principal called to tell her they were sending her teenage son home because of a behavioral problem. She went on to say that the problem had been brewing for quite a while, and she was very frustrated because her son was capable of becoming a straight-A student, but he refused to apply himself.

Although it was probably none of my business, I asked her how she planned to deal with the situation. She told me she intended to sit down at the kitchen table that evening with her husband and her son, and they were going to work out a solution to the problem once and for all. Then she asked me what I thought. Since she had attended one of my seminars, she was familiar with the PRAM Model, so I referred to it in structuring my response. I pointed out that although the method by which she planned to resolve the problem seemed very logical to her, in reality she was trying to throw an agreement formation (step three) solution at a relationship (step two) problem. I went on to tell her that although I didn't want to be the one to deliver the bad news, it was my assessment that her son didn't feel comfortable with his parents.

At first this woman became rather defensive at the notion that her son didn't feel comfortable with her and pointed out that the three members of her family had lived together for 14 years. How could they not feel comfortable with each other? I asked if she ever visited her son in his room. She responded that she did so at least a half-dozen times a week. I asked if most of the visits were pleasant and relaxed or confrontational in nature: Did she ask him things like "How come your room is such a mess?" and "You promised you'd mow the lawn yesterday—why isn't it done?" and "When are you going to get your act together at school?"

She quickly admitted that almost all her visits to her son's room were confrontational in nature. I pointed out that since this was the case, most likely her son didn't even like it when she entered his room because he knew it would be an unpleasant experience. She asked me what she should do. My response was that until the trust level was raised and her son felt good and comfortable with his parents, there would be no progress with his behavior at school. So I recommended that she and her husband work on the trust problem first. I suggested they each spend 15 minutes alone with their son every night for the following two weeks, talking about whatever their son wanted to talk about, without hassling him about anything. I asked them not to bring up the school problem until after these two weeks were over and to avoid any other types of confrontations with him during that period. In addition, I also asked them to go out of their way on a couple of occasions to make their son feel special.

Ten days later, I received a phone call from this woman to confirm my speaking date in Tucson. When we had finished talking business, I asked her how the family situation was going. She told me that both she and her husband had done exactly what I had recommended. She did admit, however, that it had taken her a few evenings to get used to going into her son's room and not hassling him. They also had gone out of their way to make him feel special by taking him to an electronics show that he was very interested in. She went on to say that as a result of all this, the problem at school had taken care of itself. It was never even brought up. She also told me that on the previous day, her son had come home from school and said to her, "Guess what happened in school today, Mom?" She said that he hadn't said anything like that since the first grade!

As this example illustrates, amazing results can be achieved in solving problems when you apply an appropriate solution to the true problem. The key to realizing such results is to diagnose the cause of the problem correctly *before* your attempt to apply a solution. And it's the PRAM Model that holds the key to an accurate diagnosis.

Cold Sales Calls

Cold calls are first-time calls on new prospects. Salespeople by and large do not like making cold calls. In fact, many of them absolutely hate it. The reason is that cold calls have such a high failure or rejection rate associated with them. As Tom Peters said in *Thriving on Chaos,* "Anyone who's been a salesperson for even a day agrees that there's no lousier way to live than depending on cold calls."

Cold calls have such a high failure rate because of the philosophy underlying the traditional approach to selling; that is "The name of the game is to *get the order.*" Adherence to this philosophy has led to a belief that the success of a sales call is judged based on whether the salesperson got the order. For this reason, salespeople operating under the traditional approach to selling feel duty-bound to push for the order whenever they make a sales call, including a cold call.

The PRAM Model provides us with insight as to why this approach results in such a high failure rate. The problem with cold calls is that no relationship, and hence no trust, exists between the salesperson and the customer. By pushing for the order in the absence of such trust, the salesperson is telling the customer that he or she is more interested in the customer's money than in the customer's welfare. Because no one likes to do business with a hustler, the customer generally says no, which the salesperson interprets as rejection or failure.

The thing to keep in mind if you want to become a highly successful salesperson is that you are after the *business* and not merely the order. Your objective is to turn a new prospect eventually into a *loyal* customer and hence a long-term source of repeat and referral business. Doing this requires that you first build a relationship between yourself and the customer *before* you try to sell him or her anything. Thus, on a first-time call, your goal should not be to sell the customer anything, but rather to initiate a relationship. Subsequent visits should be used as opportunities to cultivate the relationship and demonstrate that you are genuinely interested in the customer and his or her welfare. As Joe Gandolfo put it in his book, *How to Make Big Money Selling*, "Every supersuccessful salesperson that I've ever met comes across as a thoughtful, loving, caring individual who knows inner peace. It's a tough image to fake! . . . You've got to project sincerity and put the customer's interests first. Study successful salespeople. Their customers *always* come first. With this approach, the money automatically comes. But when the money is put first, success is usually a long way down the road."

A number of my clients have rewritten the job descriptions of their salespeople. As part of these new job descriptions, cold calling, with its unpleasant rejection rate, has been replaced with *relationship calling*: Salespeople in these organizations are expected to spend a certain percentage of their time initiating and cultivating relationships with new prospects, without the pressure of having to make an immediate sale. The reward structure in these organizations has also been expanded—it's no longer based totally on the amount of sales for a given period but now includes incentives for relationship-building activities and for sales obtained as a result of repeat and referral business. These revised job descriptions and expanded reward systems are consistent with what Tom Peters prescribed in *Thriving on Chaos*: "Sales commissions and/or salaries ought to be skewed substantially toward incentives for repeat and add-on business. . . . Repeat and add-on business usually results from a host of small but, in total, time-consuming touches. . . . Our incentives should say unequivocally, 'Spend the Time!' "

Irate Customers

Most salespeople would agree that dealing with an irate customer is, at best, an unpleasant experience. Customers who are upset can be very animated, vocal, and emotional. For this reason, many salespeople would rather avoid confrontations with an irate customer, choosing instead to write the person off as a lost cause. Highly successful salespeople, on the other hand, have found that once you understand the motivation behind the customer's irate behavior, it's not at all unpleasant to deal with it. In fact, highly successful salespeople view dealing with an irate customer as a golden opportunity to sell this person for life and to turn him or her into an active evangelist on the salesperson's behalf.

Once again, the PRAM Model provides us with insight. When a customer becomes upset, it's generally because the person's expectations of what was to happen after he or she reached an agreement with you were not met. Irate behavior on the part of a customer is therefore a *maintenance* issue. The key in dealing with irate customers is for you not to take it personally. You would probably react in a similar manner if you were in the customer's shoes.

More importantly, however, try to keep in mind that these unmet expectations also represent a blow to the customer's ego. He or she bought a product or service from you with the expectation you would deliver what you had promised, and now it seems you let him or her down. What you need to do to rectify the situation is to restore the customer's ego by showing that you still really care. You can do this by taking swift and decisive action to right the situation to the total satisfaction of the customer.

What's especially effective is to shock the irate customer a bit with how well you respond. True, it might cost you a few extra dollars, but it will buy you tons of loyalty and it will give these customers a reason to spread the word on your behalf. As Tom Peters wrote in *Thriving on Chaos*, "A well-handled problem usually breeds more loyalty than you had before the negative incident." Very often, properly taking care of disappointed customers is what will set you apart from the masses.

One Reason Why There Aren't More Millionaires

Several years ago, when I was conducting a seminar in Omaha, one of the participants stood up and asked, "If the PRAM Model is so simple and works so well, how come there aren't more millionaires?" I must admit the question caught me by surprise, so I immediately called for a break so that I could think about the answer. As I mulled this question over in my mind, it began to occur to me that the reason there aren't more millionaires, or highly successful people in any endeavor for that matter, is that most people don't recognize the importance that relationships play in being successful in any profession. These people don't devote any effort toward developing these necessary relationships because they don't see the need. Without these relationships, however, they are unable to enlist the active support of other people on their behalf and so are destined to go through life trying to do everything by themselves.

Not long ago, I gave a speech to a group of people in Atlanta, and as I talked about this very issue, I noticed a woman in the audience who was reacting with enthusiasm. When my speech was over, she came up to me, shook my hand, and said, "Please forgive me for being so excited, but my father is a self-made millionaire, and there isn't a day that goes by when he doesn't get at least one phone call from someone asking if there is anything they can do for him. I thought you would want to know that your formula works!"

On my return trip from Atlanta to Phoenix I had to change planes in Dallas. As I took my seat, I recognized the person sitting next to me.

His name was Bill King, and he was the owner of a very successful chain of brake repair shops known as Bill King's Brake-O. I had seen him many times in his television commercials.

As the two of us got to know each other, Bill King began to share with me his philosophy on success. At one point, he leaned back and said, "Ross, let me tell you from personal experience that the road to becoming a millionaire is so simple that it boggles most people's minds."

I thought to myself, Mr. King you keep talking, because I am taking notes!

He went on, "If you develop a sense of trust with your employees [relationships] and take good care of them [maintenance], your employees will take good care of you. Furthermore, if you develop a sense of trust with your customers [relationships] and take good care of them [maintenance], your customers will take good care of you." He then said, "If you want to make a million dollars a year, you need a million friends each turning a dollar a year for you. Or, you need a half-million friends each turning you two dollars per year, and so forth. If you work this process long enough, you'll eventually develop enough friends who each generate the right amount of revenue on your behalf. Once that happens," he concluded, "becoming a millionaire is a piece of cake."

I remember saying, "No wonder wealthy people don't seem to work so hard!"

Bill King laughed at my remark because he had just spent several days participating in a celebrity golf tournament. He did say, however, that developing all these necessary relationships doesn't happen overnight. It takes time, and it's work. On the other hand, it has a virtually guaranteed pay-off. Take care of the people who stand between you and success or failure, and they will take care of you.

Three Factors That Assure Your Success in Taming the X-Factor

In order for the PRAM Model to deliver the extraordinary results that are promised in this book, it must be applied within the context of three very important factors. These are *balance, integrity*, and *patience*. Applying the PRAM Model within the context of these three factors virtually assures your success in taming the X-Factor. If you ignore these concepts, you can expect ordinary results at best.

Balance

As you look at the PRAM Model, one of the things you will notice is that each of the four steps is equal in size. This means that each of the four steps is of equal importance. This does not mean that each of the four steps will take the same amount of time, but it does mean that you can't afford to ignore or skip any of these steps if you expect to achieve a high level of success. Look at the PRAM Model as if it were a baseball diamond. If you want to make a score, two things are essential. First, you must touch all four bases, and second, *you must touch them in the correct order* (Plans, Relationships, Agreements, and Maintenance). One of the more common management problems today is ignoring Step Two (Relationships) and trying to go from Step One (Plans) directly to Step Three (Agreements). Doing so virtually guarantees *ordinary* results.

A number of years ago, I gave a talk to the minor league scouting staff of the Chicago Cubs baseball team. When I had concluded my talk, I asked these people to share some of the problems

they encountered in trying to sign high school recruits. These scouts told me that the biggest problem they faced was the increased competition they
were getting from colleges and universities trying
to recruit the same players. They made it very
clear that they did not want to lure away kids who
would benefit from attending a college or university. They were concerned with those who were
not ready for college and who would be better off
going directly from high school to a minor league
baseball team.

They did admit they had relatively little problem
signing a first-, second-, or third-round draft choice
because, at the time, they could pay these people
anywhere from $60,000 to $150,000 per year. The
problem was with the lower-round draft choices. For
example, a twelfth-round draft choice received only
$700 per month and $12 per day for meal money.
On the other hand, a college scholarship could be
worth as much as $25,000 per year, depending on
the institution, and colleges and universities paid
$15 per day for meal money.

The scouts went on about how more money
would solve the problem. Finally, I suggested that
they might be attempting to throw a Step Three
(Agreements) solution at a Step Two (Relationships) problem. I said it looked to me as though
the colleges and universities weren't winning the
recruiting war against them with more money.
Rather, they were doing a better job of building

relationships with the players. I pointed out that these college coaches probably came across as big brother or father figures, and the players on these college teams probably seemed to be a great bunch of guys to hang around with. If this were the case, making more money available for minor league salaries was not going to solve their problem.

As I finished my statement, three senior scouts stood up and enthusiastically confirmed my assessment. They went on to say that in years past they had made it a point to build relationships with every young man they were even remotely interested in, because it was an open market and a high school graduate could sign with any team. Under such circumstances, it was very important to develop relationships—a high school recruit generally signed with the team whose scouting staff he felt most comfortable with. Recently, however, high school recruiting had become subject to a draft, and the player could sign only with the team that drafted him. Most scouting personnel no longer see a need to develop relationships with all the players that they might be interested in because there is only a 1-in-30 chance that they will be able to draft any one of them. Relationship building was no longer a high priority for most scouts.

One of these senior scouts, however, said that he had continued his relationship-building activities in spite of the draft. As a result, he rarely loses a player that he recruits to a college or university. He then went on to explain his method of building relationships with high school baseball players. He holds baseball clinics on Saturdays throughout his territory during the warm-weather months. He enlists the support of some former major league ball players, and then he invites approximately 30 to 40 boys to participate in each clinic. At these clinics, this scout provides instruction on some of the finer points of hitting and playing defense. These players are then given a chance to try out these new ideas in a game among themselves.

In addition to assessing each boy's potential, the goal of this scout in putting on these clinics is to make sure that he or one of his assistants interacts with each boy individually in a very positive way. For example, he told of a boy who, while batting, popped the ball straight up in the air for an out. At this point the scout halted the game and told the boy that the reason he popped the ball up was because he dipped his shoulder when he swung at the ball. He asked this boy to come back and take a few more swings while concentrating on keeping his shoulders square. After a couple of pitches, this boy was hitting the ball squarely and was very impressed that this man had taken the time to correct the problem. The scout then went over to the sideline where a pitcher was warming up. He asked the pitcher if he would like to learn how to throw a split-fingered fastball. The boy nodded, and the scout proceeded to show him the finer points of how to throw the pitch. This boy, too, was very impressed that a scout for a major league team would take the time to give him some special attention. Because of all this positive attention, at the end of the clinic, the enthusiastic consensus among the boys was, "We sure hope the Cubs draft us, because we want to play baseball for the Cubs!"

This scout did not view his job as ending once he got a recruit to say yes to the Cubs. He went on to point out that there was still more a scout could do to make his job easier. (He was referring to the Maintenance step of the PRAM Model.) He kept very close track of all the players in his territory who had been drafted and signed, and he periodically followed up to make sure that things were going well and that the Cubs were honoring all the promises he had made to them. By effectively performing this maintenance activity, he was able to turn these former recruits into a sales force on his behalf. The word got back to the high schools in his territory that the Cubs were a good team to play for and that he was a good person to deal with. This made his future recruiting efforts even easier. This renewed emphasis on relationships paid off quickly in terms of *extraordinary* results; two years later two Cub recruits were number one and two in terms of the votes they received for National League rookie of the year.

Integrity

In order for the PRAM Model to deliver the results that I have promised, it has to be applied with genuine integrity. Trying to use the PRAM Model to manipulate people will eventually expose you as a fraud, which means that no one is going to get excited about helping you achieve extraordinary results.

During my last year as a professor of management at Arizona State University, the faculty development office undertook a project to assist faculty members who were not good performers in the classroom to become better teachers. The project involved, first, identifying the 75 best teachers on the ASU campus. Next, a representative of the faculty development office was to administer a questionnaire to the students in each of these 75 teachers' classes. The instructions asked the students to evaluate their professors on a number of items such as level of preparation, enthusiasm for the subject, and so forth.

After the questionnaires had been administered, they were collected and the data run through a computer in order to find out at which of the items each professor was highly successful. Once this was known, a representative from the faculty development office interviewed each faculty member who participated in the study in an attempt to find out what he or she did that made him or her so successful. The idea was to compile the results in the form of a handbook that would serve as a guide to help the less effective teachers improve themselves.

I was fortunate enough to be included among the 75 best teachers at ASU. Six weeks after the questionnaires were administered, a person from the faculty development office showed up at my office to go over the results with me. This turned out to be a very pleasant experience for me, as she pointed out that I had scored very well. What she said next, however, really caught my attention because it revealed to me the ultimate secret to being highly successful at any people-oriented profession or activity.

She said there was one item that stood out from all the rest. This was that my students had the idea that I genuinely cared about them. As she told me this, she looked at me and said, "Now I want to know how you pulled that off!"

Since the question caught me off guard, I really didn't have an answer. I did, however, inform her of some of the things I did for my students—such as helping those who were interested become straight-A students, helping them find high-paying jobs after they graduated, and treating them like friends instead of second-class citizens. After she thought for a moment, she looked up and said, "What you're telling me is you really do care—and it shows." I must admit this comment took me by surprise because it had never occurred to me before. Yes, I did care, but caring was something I did as a matter of course with everyone. I had been taught to do so by my parents, and I didn't know any other way to operate.

Reflecting back on my 10 years as a professor at ASU, I remember receiving a lot of good-natured kidding from some of my colleagues. Some of them told me I spent far too much time with my students. Others told me that my salary level didn't warrant my giving those students the level of service that I did. I would acknowledge their comments and point out that it was the one aspect of my job that I really enjoyed. Interestingly enough, when I resigned my position and went into business for myself, my income immediately tripled, and 80 percent of my business during the first two years I was out on my own came from my ex-students. Until then, I had never associated the idea of caring about people as having any sort of payoff, but it really does. What goes around definitely does come around. When you really care, what comes back is always more than what you gave away in the first place. Caring still pays off for me today, in that nearly 100 percent of my consulting, speaking, and training business is the result of repeat business and referrals. As you can see, caring really does pave the way for *extraordinary* results.

Patience

Whenever we apply any new management tech-
nique or process, most of us expect instant results.
The continued popularity of fad diets serves as an
indicator of this quick-fix mentality. This final concept, patience, is probably the most difficult to apply. The PRAM Model is so much more than a
quick fix. Rather, it's a *sure* fix and a *lasting* fix. Yes,
it does produce instant results, but, more importantly, it also produces phenomenal results over the
long term.

You can only reap the full benefits of taming the
X-Factor *after* you've taken someone through all
four steps of the PRAM Model. Furthermore, you
must take each person through the PRAM Model
one step at a time over a period of time. You can't
expect all this to happen in one or two quick visits
any more than you can expect to make a serious
marriage commitment after one or two half-hour
dates. That's not the way people work. Developing
trust takes time and has to occur at a natural and
comfortable pace.

Shortly after I returned from Vietnam, I entered
the doctoral program in business administration at
Michigan State University. As the money I received
from the G.I. Bill covered only a fraction of the cost
of going to school, I joined an Army Reserve unit in
order to make up the difference. I was then given
command of the unit, which meant that I was re-

sponsible for everything regarding that unit, including recruiting.

The unit I took over was supposed to have 104 people in it. After I performed a personnel audit, I found that it had only 54 people on its rolls. In addition, 26 of these 54 were getting out of the Army Reserve within six months. The biggest reason people joined reserve units during the Vietnam era was to avoid the draft, and the draft had just ended. Just when I thought things couldn't get any worse, the next day a general from Indianapolis came up and informed me that if I didn't bring my unit up to full strength within six months, I would be relieved of my command.

At this point, I really wanted to tell this insensitive general what he could do with his reserve unit, but my reputation was important to me and I didn't want a black mark on my service record. So I decided I would give it a go and try to recruit the necessary 76 people. Talk about a tough sell! Just try to get someone to sign up to be hassled at least one weekend a month and two weeks each summer for six years, when there is no draft, in the relatively small city of Lansing, Michigan, just as the Vietnam war is winding down and antimilitary sentiment is high. Even if someone were to take you up on such a deal, you'd have to question his sanity!

However, I decided to take recruiting these 76 people as a personal challenge. I started by ensuring that I was taking very good care of the people who were already in my unit in the hope that some of them would reenlist or bring their friends. This meant straightening out any pay problems without delay, making sure we had warm tents and hot food when we went to the field, seeing to it that people were promoted on time or even ahead of time if they deserved it, and in general going to bat for them when they encountered problems. I also took a personal interest in each individual. We spent a lot of time after meetings talking about careers and what the future might hold in store for each of us.

I took a similar approach with potential new recruits. Instead of trying to sign them up immediately, I got to know them first. I also made it a point to go to their homes and get to know members of their families. In a number of cases, these potential recruits would have a friend or two at their homes when I made these visits. We would talk about the future, about the army, or about anything else these people were interested in, but I never tried to sell people on signing up for the Army Reserve while I was on one of these visits. All this visiting did consume a large amount of time, but I enjoyed getting to know all these people. I wasn't sure if there was going to be a payoff, because during the first four and a half months, I recruited only 11 people. But during the next six weeks, 71 people signed up! It was amazing. One person walked into my office with 13 of his friends, all of whom wanted to enlist in my unit. A dozen others brought at least one friend with them when they signed up.

If you observed what went on during only those last six weeks, it looked like I had a natural gift for attracting people and selling to them. They came in from all directions almost begging for a chance to become part of my unit. What wouldn't have been apparent, however, was that during the preceding four and a half months I took nearly every one of those people through all four steps of the PRAM Model, one step at a time. Yes, it was a lot of work and took a lot of time, but the payoff was *extraordinary!*

Index

About the Author

Ross R. Reck, Ph.D., is an internationally known author, consultant, and speaker. He is coauthor of *The Win-Win Negotiator*. This best-selling book has been described as a breakthrough for understanding and conducting the negotiation process. Because of its universe appeal, *The Win-Win Negotiator* has been translated into four additional languages (German, Japanese, Portuguese, and Spanish).

A compelling and dynamic speaker, Dr. Reck has been featured at hundreds of meetings, conferences, and conventions. In addition, he has consulted extensively throughout the United States, Canada, Europe, and Asia. Recent clients include Hewlett-Packard, John Deere, Hoechst Marion Roussel, Immunex, American Express, Janssen-Ortho, and Xerox.

Dr. Reck received his Ph.D. from Michigan State University in 1977. From 1975 to 1985, he served as a Professor of Management at Arizona State University. While at ASU, he became the only two-time recipient of the prestigious "Teaching Excellence in Continuing Education" award and was identified by the university as an "Outstanding Teacher." Since 1985, he has dedicated his full-time efforts to positioning his clients for new heights of achievement.

Inquiries regarding Dr. Reck's availability to speak to your group, meeting, conference, or convention should be directed to:

Ross Reck & Associates
P.O. Box 26264
Tempe, AZ 85285-6264
(480) 820-7700
reckpram@aol.com